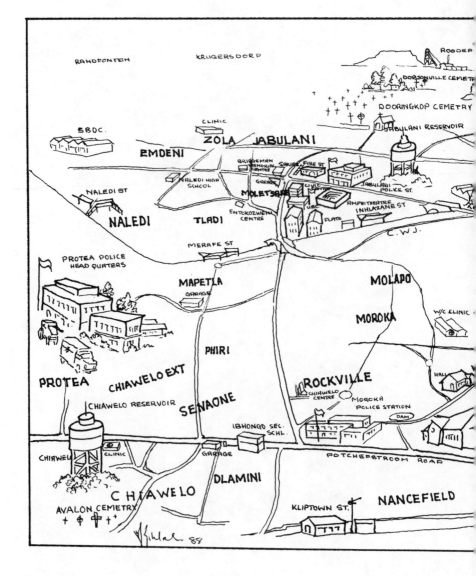

South Africa: Diary of Troubled Times

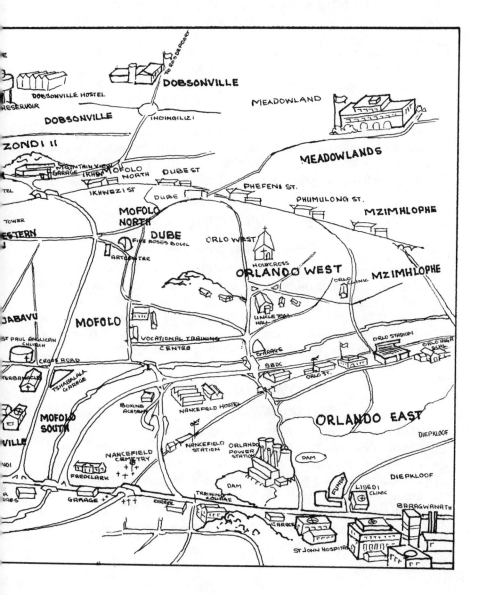

FREEDOM HOUSE

Freedom House is an independent nonprofit organization that monitors human rights and political freedom around the world. Established in 1941, Freedom House believes that effective advocacy of civil rights at home and human rights abroad must be grounded in fundamental democratic values and principles.

In international affairs, Freedom House continues to focus attention on human rights violations by oppressive regimes, both of the left and the right. At home, we stress the need to guarantee all citizens not only equal rights under law, but equal opportunity for social and economic advancement.

Freedom House programs and activities include bimonthly and annual publications, conferences and lecture series, public advocacy, ongoing research of political and civil liberties around the globe, and selected, on-site monitoring to encourage fair elections.

FOCUS ON ISSUES

General Editor: James Finn

This publication is one in a series of Focus on Issues. The separate publications in this series differ in the method of examination and breadth of the study, but each focuses on a single, significant political issue of our time. The series represents one aspect of the extensive program of Freedom House. The views expressed are those of the authors and not necessarily those of the Board of Freedom House.

ABOUT THE AUTHOR

Currently assistant editor of *Frontline* magazine (Johannesburg), Nomavenda Mathiane was born in Venda "Homeland" of Zulu parents. Her family moved to Johannesburg (Soweto) in the early 1950s and Ms. Mathiane was educated in Pretoria. She began her journalistic career in 1972 at Drum Publications and since then has written for numerous publications, including *World*, the *Voice* and the *Star*. Her very personal and acute observations and her frequently sharp and unconventional views have won for Ms. Mathiane an ever-widening and appreciative audience. She has two daughters and one son.

South Africa: Diary of Troubled Times

Nomavenda Mathiane

Focus on Issues, No. 7

Freedom House

First published 1989.

Cover design by Emerson Wajdowicz Studios, N.Y.C.
Cover photograph by Alf Khumalo.
Artist's eye view of Soweto by Durand Sihlali.
Inside photographs by Leonard R. Sussman.

Library of Congress Cataloging-in-Publication Data

Mathiane, Nomavenda.
    South Africa :   diary of troubled times.

    (Focus on issues ; no. 7)
    1. Soweto (South Africa)—Social conditions.
2. Blacks—South Africa—Soweto—Social conditions.
3-Apartheid—South Africa—Soweto. 4. Soweto
(South Africa)—Politics and government. I. Title.
II. Series: Focus on issues (Freedom House (U.S.)) ; 7.
DT944.J66S6824   1988   968.2'21   88-33590
ISBN 0-932088-38-4
ISBN 0-932088-37-6   (pbk.)

Distributed by arrangement with
National Book Network
4720 Boston Way
Lanham, MD 20706

3 Henrietta Street
London, WC2E 8LU England

Contents

South Africa:
Diary of Troubled Times

Introduction

REALITY'S CONTOURS HAVE too many rough edges to fit the Procrustean bed of the dogmatist. So in times of social turmoil, we need factual accounts of events on the ground as an antidote to the distortions and oversimplifications of ideologues.

Nomavenda Mathiane's graphic essays on the everyday tribulations of black South Africans in the twenty-six townships that constitute Soweto, just outside Johannesburg, qualify as such an antidote.

A black journalist for *Frontline*, an independent South African journal that has published most of the pieces appearing here, Mathiane—one of Soweto's approximately 2 million inhabitants—knows that the ultimate source of South Africa's woes is the system of apartheid. She writes that "as long as blacks are not part of the governing body, and as long as the law is designed by whites without blacks...then hope and security for this country will remain a pipe dream."

This is the most basic political truth about South Africa, but it is also the most obvious one. What Mathiane deserves special credit for is her recognition that the incendiary, violent militance of some of apartheid's opponents is not the answer to apartheid but, rather, another of its awful consequences. She sees that violence begets violence, and that ideological fanaticism begets its mirrored counterpart.

The real value of Mathiane's essays, though, lies less in her opinions, acute as they are, than in the portrait of social upheaval that she conveys.

Written from 1985 to 1988, the pieces depict a Soweto gone awry—where murder, assault, arson, intimidation and fear often seem to be the rule, not the exception; and, most strikingly, where the collapse of the collaborationist local government has created a vacuum of authority within which adolescent activists often dictate the political agenda to their parents.

The poignant fact is that within Soweto these matters usually involve black against black. The feared police sometimes come out to hunt for activists; and when there is a rent boycott, distant and faceless whites shut off the electricity and water in retaliation. But on an immediate, day-to-day basis, it is the black (and mostly young) militants, not whites, who most make their presence felt in Soweto's constituent townships.

As Mathiane makes unmistakably clear, many if not most of the residents of Soweto are too terrified to defy the township militants, who generally identify with the exiled African National Congress (ANC) and the United Democratic Front (UDF), which many regard as the ANC's internal ally. In her words: "People have opted for popularity with the students, because opposing them is to invite being necklaced."

So although many resent the school boycott for depriving their children of an education (especially the poorest people, who can't send their children to private schools), they comply with it, just as they continue the rent boycott—death, after all, is more fearsome than either ignorance or eviction.

It's not that Sowetans have anything but loathing for apartheid. In fact, they pride themselves on being tougher and more defiant than blacks elsewhere in the country. It's just that they wish that their leaders, whether in the ANC or the Azanian People's Organization—Azapo, the standard bearer of the Black Consciousness Movement movement, with which Mathiane identifies—would shape their strategies in ways that are more constructive and less likely to produce unnecessary deaths. Mathiane succinctly dismisses the ideologues who claim (as far left and far right ideologues all over the world do) that those who don't follow them 100 percent of the time are sellouts: "There is a myth that because we are anti-government, therefore we must unquestioningly be pro any measure imposed by the movements...We are against the government and the System and are also against school boycotts and necklacing."

The gap between leaders and their not-always-willing followers raises a key question too often overlooked by well-meaning Americans and Europeans. Can the fight against apartheid be conducted so that the racial caste system is toppled peacefully and is followed by democracy, not another form of tyranny? Liberals often state (correctly) that it isn't enough to be anti-Communist; that one must offer a positive, democratic alternative to Communism. Would that they also recognized that being anti-apartheid isn't sufficient.

At any rate, to deal with this question we need to backtrack a bit and briefly examine South African history over the last dozen years or so.

Mathiane often refers to June 1976, and well she might; for it was then that Soweto gained world renown as it ushered in a new era in South African history. During that month a school boycott, initiated by Sowetan students against the teaching of the Afrikaans language, erupted into violence when the police tried to end it by force. By the time the ensuing strife in Soweto and elsewhere subsided, over 500 people had been killed, many of them children. Since then, it has been clear that never again could the South African government count on the quiet acceptance of apartheid by blacks.

Relative tranquility prevailed for a while, but late in 1984 a new, longer, more intense and more widespread upheaval began.

This time the most proximate cause was the elections held under the country's new constitution, which for the first time gave Indians and persons of mixed race the opportunity to elect their own chambers of a tripartite Parliament. The system was rigged so that the white chamber would dominate, and the great majority of Indians and mixed race South Africans did not vote. But for blacks, the new dispensation made their own total lack of political power even more galling than before.

Black protest since then has taken many forms, including resistance to forced eviction from zones designated for whites under the Group Areas Act, school boycotts, consumer boycotts of white-owned stores, rent boycotts and labor strikes. Clashes between blacks and the police and soldiers have resulted in many hundreds of deaths; at the politicized funerals for the victims to which Mathiane refers, new clashes have often added to the death toll.

In July 1985 President Pieter Botha declared a state of emergency, which has been renewed every year since. Violence has declined significantly since then, but South African society is more polarized than it was several years ago—what exists now is not peace but a truce that no sensible person can expect will last.

In fact, since 1985 a trend toward loosening the chains of oppression has become endangered. In 1979, the ruling National Party passed legislation allowing black workers to organize trade unions and strike. Also, in the late 1970s and early 1980s, the government began to modify the apartheid system to eliminate some of its most visible components, such as segregated public accommodations.

But the turmoil of the last few years threatens even these gains. Legislation restricting the workers' right to strike and organize has been passed. In the 1987 national election the ultra-right Conservative Party replaced the liberal, anti-apartheid Progressive Federal Party as the largest opposition group in the white chamber of Parliament. In 1988, the Conservatives made considerable gains in municipal elections and were preparing to resegregate public accommodations in the localities that they controlled. Meanwhile ANC bombings, originally limited to military targets and economically strategic sites, now hit civilian targets such as soccer stadiums and shopping malls.

This is such a bleak picture that at first glance we might be tempted to conclude that there is no chance for a peaceful transition to democracy. If the externally based military forces of the ANC are the only hope for ending apartheid, then this would certainly be the case. But in the last decade there has been a proliferation in black South Africa of such democratic institutions as trade unions, student and cultural organizations, religious groups, and street committees. Most of these types of organizations can play a direct role in resisting apartheid. Also, and at least as importantly, all of them function as democratically based models and training grounds for a future South African policy.

4

Let's examine two types of groups that appear in Mathiane's essays: trade unions and street committees.

Despite recent restrictions on the right to organize and strike, black South Africans have two strong union federations—the National Council of Trade Unions (NACTU) and the Congress of South African Trade Unions (COSATU)—as well as a number of strong independent unions. While NACTU is aligned with the Black Consciousness movement and COSATU is linked to the ANC, both are powerful institutions in their own right and not simply the pawns of ideologues. They are currently working on a joint strategy to contend with the new restrictions. Meanwhile, some of their constituent unions are pressuring employers to sign agreements that put aside many of the restrictions. The Garment and Allied Workers Union has already forced employers to agree not to implement those clauses of the restrictive legislation that it finds most offensive.

The significance of the labor movement for blacks is illustrated by Mathiane's essay on a railway strike. One striker told her that if he lost his job as a result of the strike, he would have difficulty getting another one because of his age. Since his family was entirely dependent on him, his children would have to leave school and look for work. But, he said: "I got a lot of strength from my colleagues during the strike...We were all not sure if it was the right thing to do and there were times when we would be on the verge of breaking, but...at the meetings, the leaders would revive our flagging spirits, telling us that victory was in sight."

The leaders were right: the railway workers won a large wage increase. In the broader picture, this kind of experience reinforces a sense of personal worth and provides valuable lessons in the value and methods of cooperative struggle. And since South Africa is by far the most industrialized nation in Africa, trade union democracy can play a larger role in shaping that nation's future than it has anywhere else on the continent.

With the collapse of white-established local governments in 1985 and 1986, urban blacks formed street committees in Soweto and elsewhere. Both the ANC and the South African government insist that these committees are revolutionary organizations allied with

5

the ANC's armed struggle. On the face of it this seems more like fantasy than reality, since the violence in South Africa has not had the marks of organization or coordination.

Mathiane's reports on street committees in Soweto confirm our suspicions. She acknowledges that while some committees sprung up spontaneously to reestablish order, others were formed by the young militants who then used them to rule through intimidation. But even in these cases, she reports, "It is clear that a process is under way that has a momentum of its own—the passing of power from ideologues to the hands of genuine community leaders." In one case, adults insisted on a secret ballot and, by this means, displaced the hard-line students from the leadership. (In fact, the vote was so lopsided that most of the students must have voted against their fellows.)

On another street, the militants called the residents together to form a committee. One after another of the fearful inhabitants made lame excuses for not serving as the executive. Finally, one of them agreed, with a qualification: "Our politics are no longer run democratically. If you disagree with the crowd, you get necklaced. If I am called to agree to that, I want to tell you here and now that I will stop being chairman of this committee." The militants agreed.

On examples of courage such as these rest in large part the hopes for peace and democracy in South Africa.

Ultimately, what happens in South Africa is up to South Africans. But if any outside force can have some impact on the course of events, it is the United States, with its economic power and its moral influence as the leader of the democratic nations.

The South African government is moving to the right under Conservative Party pressure and is taking back some of the concessions it has made to anti-apartheid sentiment. Therefore, counterpressure from the United States might be of particular value now. The Reagan administration's so-called contructive engagement policy should be abandoned by President Bush. South African whites, who almost never have to visit black communities and who are sheltered from the sight of violence by state censorship, have ostrich-like proclivities when it comes to assessing their society and the world. Aside from improving our image in the eyes of black

South Africans, a more forthright U.S. policy might force whites to recognize the costs of apartheid.

As an example of private efforts, the AFL-CIO and the A. Philip Randolph Institute work with and support South Africa's black trade unions. American professional, student, religious, educational and other organizations should follow this example by linking up with their counterparts in the black townships. If substantial and lasting change in South Africa can come only from within, then support for these institutions is the most positive contribution that we can make to a nonviolent, democratic future for that country.

NORMAN HILL, PRESIDENT
A. PHILIP RANDOLPH INSTITUTE,
A. PHILIP RANDOLPH EDUCATIONAL FUND

Labor Pains

I GOT INTO the taxi and sat next to a pregnant woman, a picture of health. She sat there demurely displaying her happy and healthy state of well-being. For a moment I envied her contented appearance and wished her well.

The taxi went on collecting people. Soon it was full and on its way to town. I had forgotten about my neighbor when she nudged me and whispered, "I am not feeling too well." She moved slightly forward and balanced her hand on her hip. I closed the magazine I had been reading, and looked into her face. I don't know what I was looking for, but I didn't find it. I looked at my watch, the way midwives do. It was just after 7:30 A.M. I leaned toward her and asked her when she was due. She mumbled, "Next month." I asked her if it was her first baby she was carrying. She told me it was the second. We went on chatting about pregnancies and children and related matters.

Ten minutes later she grimaced and held on to her knee. I feared the worst was about to happen. I held her hand and told her not to worry, we would soon be in town and I would ask the driver to take her to the hospital. I also said she need not worry much, as it might be just a false alarm. I felt good. I had used midwives' jargon. Clever.

Another pain struck. She held tightly on to my hand. I looked around and counted the women in the taxi—three. The rest were men, eight including the driver. She put her handbag on the floor and moved forward as if to give herself more room to breathe. Fanning herself with one hand and holding on to her knee with the other, she seemed to be in immense pain. I beckoned to one of the women and told her the problem. The man seated in front of me understood what was going on from our looks and exchanged seats with the woman whose help I was enlisting. No questions were asked as we sat watching the woman writhe in pain. Beads of sweat were running down her face. She no longer seemed to be conscious of her surroundings. The man next to us moved to give his seat to the other woman. The four of us sat there agonizing. Someone told the driver what was happening and he reduced speed. All was quiet in the minibus. We were in the middle of nowhere.

Helplessly we watched cars drive past and wondered what we were going to do about the woman giving birth. We were now on the highway to town when the driver suddenly moved to the extreme left lane, crossed the yellow line and parked his vehicle. We transferred the woman to the back seat. One of the women started stroking the woman's belly while someone suggested we stop one of the passing cars and ask them to call for an ambulance. The driver got out to seek help.

Although the men would not look at what was going on in the back seat, anguish was written all over their faces. "How far is she?" their faces seemed to ask, or "Can't you make it easy for her?" We stood there knowing the effort was between her and the baby, and yet we were part of it. One of the women peeked between the woman's legs and said, "She will be getting the baby in seconds now." The woman was wailing silently and praying loud. Our nerves were about to snap. The other woman kept rubbing her belly while some of us prayed.

Then she screamed. One of the older women took a peek and said, "Come on now, my child, this is it—push." The woman held on to our arms and started pushing. We were oblivious to the heavy traffic outside as we joined hands, minds and souls. I felt sweat come down my forehead and spine. I held tight to her hand as she clung to mine. She was sweating, grimacing and pushing with all her might when slowly the baby started appearing. It was like watching a movie, while at the same time being part of it, as the head gently broke out, made a turn and one by one the shoulders and wham! the legs were out. One of the women caught it, turned it upside down and gave it a slap. The little thing released such a scream. We all started. And it was over.

I'VE THOUGHT OF that morning, those many years ago, when the lives of so many strangers came to a standstill. I have thought of how the pain of birth, initially confined to the woman, had gradually engulfed the rest of us. I still carry the mental pictures of how we had wrung our hands in desperate helplessness as she writhed in agony. We prayed with her and we suffered the pain with her.

Isn't it strange that none of us, as we got into the taxi preoccupied with the thought of our various destinations, had an inkling of what would befall us? How were we to know we would be part of a happening of such importance? Isn't it true that if we had been asked as we boarded the taxi if we wanted to share in such an experience we would have refused? But we did share in it. We were destined to experience the birth in that fashion and at that particular time.

Childbirth is unique with every woman. And every child has a route and manner different from other children. They may be born of the same woman but their circumstances are not the same. Some take days while others take minutes. Who dictates? It is a struggle and nobody can decide or dictate the form, shape or duration.

I have lived with the "struggle" all my life—long before I could understand its meaning. I heard the struggle being pronounced by men at work. I have heard women mention the struggle as they carried on with their chores at home. To me, the struggle became synonymous with liberation. "When the struggle is over..." I heard as a young girl when Jomo Kenyatta was fighting the British in Kenya. I heard it when Kwame Nkruma led his people to independence in Ghana and I also heard it when he went into exile and there was talk of the country "going to the dogs." I was to hear it again at the Rivonia trial followed by the exodus of people leaving the country.

I have heard it many more times as I have grown older. At

first it was not any of my business as one by one people in the struggle were detained or died. One mourned those one knew and hoped the whole nasty business could be sorted out. Gradually, like a net, people got dragged in. It was no longer Mandela or Sobukwe on Robben Island. 1976 came and went. Maybe it was the first pains. Perhaps the false alarm. The midwives looked at their watches, peeped and went back to the waiting rooms, continued knitting and reported the patient's progress simply as "one finger dilated."

They went on with their business: crocheting and knitting and talking about their families or discussing patients. Who cares? "That woman in bed #5 is going to be here for days," they said. But the woman in bed #5 was not just lying there and enjoying the comfort of the hospital bed. The moment for her to stop everything and begin the long process of delivery had come. It was just a matter of minutes before the nurses, the doctors, as well as people at home would join her in the marvelous and painful task of bringing a life into the world. A matter of time.

DURING THE CARTER administration, a number of black congressmen visited South Africa. At an informal dinner held in their honor by one of the activists here, talk veered, of course, to South Africa's independence. Questions were thrown about and answered. Then one of the Americans, Congressman William Gray asked, "But are you blacks ready for it?" The question bordered on arrogance. Typical of all self-styled facilitators, he had given the situation a cursory peep and concluded the patient was far from delivery. But a Soweto leader, Mr. Mosala, in his gentle and wise manner of talking saved the night. "Does an expectant woman make an appointment with the baby to be born?" asked the man. While the woman may have a say insofar as conceiving, she has absolutely no say on how and when the child is to be born. How does one, therefore, say to a people, "Now get ready, a new society is about to be born?"

A new society is not born by magic. It moves at its own pace. It determines the pace. It takes shape according to the specifics of its needs. For some countries the period was much shorter. Ours seems to take an eternity. Could it be the real pains or just a false alarm that we see the South African society disintegrate, and we watch our children become aliens to us, our culture and tradition? Whether it be false or real, the fact is that something to do with a new order is happening. A new society is being born and we are all sweating, writhing and pushing.

It begins humbly with individuals. Those who conceive of the idea develop it. They get detained, skip the country, while the rest of mankind refuses even to talk about it. The architects continue while some fall by the wayside. And yet the seed already in the womb continues to grow. The individual tosses with the uncomfortable feeling of carrying. The rest of the people watch with apparent disinterest as the society changes. And soon, one by one, they begin to hold hands.

March, 1985

Pontso

I SPEND MANY a Saturday afternoon at a blind people's center in Soweto. There are three reasons for this habit. First, I admire the people who run the center for their commitment and dedication. In spite of their handicap, they go about their business professionally and efficiently, much to the shame of many organizations run by people with sight. Second, the director is a personal friend of mine. I have known her half my life. Third, and very important, the center is a sanctuary for me. I run to it for peace of mind. There, I'm surrounded by people who care and who never hesitate to show they care to all who enter their premises.

Pontso, the director and my friend, is a woman with a deep sense of responsibility. When she first expressed the idea of establishing an association for the blind, I thought she was crazy and would never get it off the ground. But she was quick to convince me, saying, "Look, I don't hope to put an end to the army of blind beggars who sit on the pavements, but I do intend to reduce their numbers drastically."

Shortly thereafter, Pontso resigned her secure job as a switchboard operator for the West Rand Board to start the Transvaal Association of the Black Blind Adult (TABBA). Without financial backing and armed only with a typewriter and commitment, she typed proposals and letters of appeal for TABBA from the small house she shares with her husband and four children. She convinced most of her relatives and friends to help make her dream come true and, indeed, a great part of it already has.

One Saturday, I was summoned by Pontso and told of her plans to start a publication for TABBA. Her assistant, Mpho, who reads to me and drives her around, was in an adjoining office with some people. From where Pontso and I sat, I could see people coming from the station or going to the taxi rank. I also noticed a group of boys milling around. Pontso meanwhile, was detailing how she thought the newsletter should be designed. It was to be in braille, of course, but also in print for the benefit of the sighted spouses and children of the blind. I sat there marvelling at the way Pontso glibly spoke of what she wanted done without having a clue about what goes on in the printing and publishing world. What bliss!

She was still at it when there was a loud banging on the door. I started, and Pontso stopped talking and turned in my direction. There was another knock. I looked out of the window and saw a group of youths on the verandah.

"Pontso, you have visitors. I think it's comrades. What could they possibly want?" The knocking was persistent.

"Let's open the door," Pontso said.

I opened the door. "What do you want?" I said. I was now accustomed to the intimidating tactics of the comrades.

Pontso had come to stand behind me and Mpho and her visitors had joined us. The two groups—one of women, the other of boys—confronted one another.

"We want Mpho to give us the car to go to a funeral vigil in Thokoza," said a boy.

What was the world coming to! Everyone knew this was a blind people's center. How on earth could these boys want the blind to sacrifice their car to them? I was disgusted. Unfortunately, being sighted, my anger was written all over my face. I looked behind to find Mpho. Her big eyes were filled with fear and looked as though they were about to jump out of their sockets.

It was Pontso who saved the situation.

"Are you going to stand there and talk to us or are you going to come in?" she asked.

One by one the boys shuffled in, found seats and made themselves comfortable.

"Yes, my boys, can I help you?" said Pontso.

"We want Mpho's car to go to the vigil tonight."

"I'm afraid, boys, Mpho doesn't own the car. The car is mine. In fact, it's not even mine but belongs to the organization."

"We don't care whose it is. In fact, we know it's a white man's car. And if you don't give it to us, we'll show you a thing or two," the leader said.

Before he could finish his sentence, another youth said, "We will kidnap Mpho's child. After all, she can always get another one from the whites, as they supply you with everything."

"I shall pretend I didn't hear that insult," Pontso said. "Tell me, boys, who do you actually work for? I mean here we are, defenseless and blind women, fighting for our survival. Now, you want to deprive us of our only means of transport? Why do you have to come to us? Can't you get other people to give you a car?"

"Look, Ma, I don't think we have the time to argue with you. Either you give us the car or we'll have to persuade you somehow. We can't sit here and listen to your problems. We have to go and bury our friend in Thokoza who was gunned down by the Boers."

"Does anyone of you have a license?" Pontso asked.

"Oh come on! Who needs a license these days?"

"Well, we need to give our car over to somebody who has a license, just in case you get involved in an accident and we need to claim. And to safeguard us in case you fail to bring the car back, we should then know whom to contact."

"Don't worry, Ma, the car will definitely come back tomorrow," a youth said.

"I'm going to go against my principles and give you the car," Pontso said. "Not because you have threatened us, but because I want you to prove your worth to me. If things weren't as bad as they are, I would not be compromised. You may take the car. I have your word that you will bring it back. I hope it amounts to something."

Mpho and I watched with anger as the youths packed into the car. Mpho regretted that she had filled it with petrol that morning. "Well, you can rest assured they will only return it, if they do, when it is empty," said Pontso.

The car was not returned.

ON MONDAY, PONTSO phoned me at the office and asked what she should do. There was no way she could report the matter to the police. That would simply incur the wrath of the comrades. And she could not stay another day without reporting its loss if she wanted the insurance company to compensate her for her loss. She was in a "Catch-22" situation.

After a lengthy conversation, we decided to solicit the help of comrades from a nearby township. I collected Pontso and we went to a student we knew was active in such matters. He was livid when we told him what had happened.

"How can people do that to you Aus Pontso? We will find them, I tell you. We'll show them a thing or two."

What did that mean, I wondered. A "necklace" or a house gutted by fire? Anyway, the matter was now beyond our control. There was still no sign of the car on Wednesday. Pontso called me again. The matter was very grave, she said. It had to be reported to the police. In the meantime, the student whose help we had sought had not come back to us. At that stage, we didn't know if the police were aware of our dilemma, and were simply waiting to hear our story. I persuaded Pontso to wait just another day. I told her that, since she had not reported the car's loss the day it was missing, there was no point now in losing sleep over the legality of failing to report the matter. She was not so much worried or scared about the law as she was angry at being grounded. She was to have attended meetings in Johannesburg and Ga-Rankuwa, but had not been able to go.

When she woke on Thursday morning, a shell of what had been her car was parked a few meters from the corner of her street. The battery, tires and a number of other items were missing. Later in the same day, she received a message from the students' movement that there would be a meeting and they wanted her to attend, as the theft of her car was on the agenda. She was reluctant to go.

"Why do I have to go," she asked. "Look at the state of the car. Do you think these kids will repay us? Why should I waste my time with such heartless kids as these?"

After a long discussion, we decided we should go and hear what the youth had to say for themselves. We could not understand their logic. They had asked for Pontso's car and promised to return it the next day. They didn't and, when they had returned it, they just dumped a wreckage on her street corner. What kind of arrogance was that?

THE MEETING HALL was filled with youth shouting slogans. Some of the songs and slogans were, although unintentionally, downright funny and I wondered how the youngsters would look at them when they became adults. I have often thought of the long way we've come. The slogans of my generation were laments for our lost land. As youngsters, we used to cry for our lost land, taken by the Boers. Later, when I started work, the slogans and songs were very abusive and called the Boers dogs. Now they have become war songs. There is no more lamenting as they go to battle.

We watched the young warriors stamping their feet and raising their fists as they crushed the enemy. It was no longer a promise or threat of "When we come back from those hills, there will be gunfire," or "Our mommys are delighted we are back." They were with Mandela on the battlefield. The leader of the students took the platform and immediately spoke of Pontso's car.

"There are some elements who are going about harassing our parents in the name of the struggle. We have invited 'Mama' here to come and tell us exactly how it happened. We are not going to have our parents living in fear because of some mad people. But more than that, these mad people must not use our name in their dirty work."

You could have knocked me down with a feather! We'd thought the boys who had come for the car were real comrades! But how were we to know they were not? Little wonder that in some areas people actually asked for identity and membership cards from comrades. Maybe we should have done that too. So much for wisdom after the fact.

The leader invited Pontso up to the platform while a song was being sung. She thanked the students for inviting her and touched on how the car was taken from her.

"But, I am not going to dwell on the inconvenience that has caused me. I think I want to use this platform to tell you about us. This is a great opportunity for me to talk to you kids and to tell you about our organization.

"A lot of harm has come to this country because people don't talk to each other and, when people stop talking, they fight. Really, how can we, you and I, fight? How can mother fight child, brother fight sister? Yet it is happening.

"Maybe the best thing to have happened to us and you this year has been the taking of our car. For had that not happened we would not be here and, as long as we work in our little corner and you in yours, we are likely to clash, as has already happened.

"Most of you know who I am. You have seen me in the street. Some of you used to see me walking home from the office where I used to work. So I don't need to tell you about myself. Our organization is called TABBA, which stands for Transvaal Association for Black Blind Adults. We are an association independent from the government welfare organization. We came into being because of a need that existed and still does and will continue for as long as the present system of government exists.

"We blind people got together and decided we needed to create an organization that would, first, offer a home for people in our position; second, that would educate ourselves about our plight; and third, that would find ways of getting out of it.

"As black people, we have the problem of being vanquished. As black blind people, we have added problems. For sighted people, being blind means a lack of sight, that's all. To us, it's more than that. So while you wage your struggle against the system, we also have ours to fight. I could speak for hours on what we go through as blind people in this country, as well as in this world, but I know there are more urgent issues that need our attention right now. In our organization, we have people who were born blind and others who were born sighted, but lost sight at some stage of their lives through illness or accident or old age. Some of these people are not only blind, but also physically handicapped in other ways.

"These are the people we have to counsel and to educate that being blind is not the end of the world, but that they are the result of the system we are all fighting.

"I am talking of young people like you who, only a few months ago, were stamping their feet as you are doing, confident about fighting the Boer to the end. They are the people who today have joined our ranks and have to fight the war from a different battle-field. In brief, that is what we are all about."

Having said that, she asked to be excused and we left the hall. As we left, we felt how angry the youth were at whoever had taken the car and we knew that, from that day onwards, they were on our side. We knew there was no way anybody posing as a comrade would want to do the organization any harm.

We learned later that night that the students had gotten hold of two of the boys who had taken the car and had beaten them to a pulp. The car, however, had to be written off.

March, 1986

Diary, Soweto

THERE ARE NOT many people in Soweto who know Bra Thabo. Those who do know he is a no-nonsense person. He takes no nonsense from his business associates or friends. If he is your friend, then you have a friend indeed. But woe to his enemies!

One of Bra Thabo's outstanding traits is his permanently immaculate state. I always tease him and say his mind is as clean as his looks. "Class, baby, class," he replies. Bra Thabo speaks very fast and is usually critical of something. I can't recall a time when he has been complimentary about anything. If you try to praise him about his business endeavors, he is quick to say, "Thanks to you blacks, you support me."

I don't always agree with him, but I have learned over the years not to argue with him; it's futile. In fact, he's a bit of a know-it-all. One of the best things about him, though, is that he produces results in everything he's engaged in. And he expects the same of everyone else. He hired a political activist for "strategic and expedient reasons," as he later put it. The guy didn't last three months.

When I asked Bra Thabo about it, he said, "Look, you people are forever complaining that 'whitey' does this and that to you. I employ a black guy with a degree and expect him to work, but what did I get? He wants to compete with me."

"I had only to turn my back and he was reading the newspaper or sitting on the telephone. Not only that, mind you. He starts criticizing my operations. I didn't hire him for that. I wanted work from him. I don't care what he thinks of me as a person and I'm not interested in his politics. We can argue politics at Regina Mundi. I pay him for a particular job and that's all I want from him.

"The trouble is that blacks want to be managers without doing anything. Is it any wonder we have so many token managers? Let me tell you something. Many people should be grateful to apartheid. There is a lot of rotten stuff on both sides of the fence."

That sums up Bra Thabo. He talks business all the time and always plans ahead. One afternoon, we were approaching his imposing bottle store when he noticed a group of youngsters with stones milling round his property. He drove straight to where the boys were and asked them what their problem was. Apologetic and trying to put their case to him, the boys said they were stoning white-owned properties in Soweto. He was livid.

"What? Who said this is a white man's business? Do you know me? I'm Bra Thabo and I own this business. And I can tell you one thing, when this building goes down, it will take a number of you down with it."

The youths shuffled and began to retreat.

"And the next time you want to burn a building you think is white-owned, do your homework boys! Otherwise you'll get into serious trouble," Bra Thabo called, making sure the boys left his property.

I asked him if he would drive me home. He hesitated, saying he didn't fancy driving deep into Soweto on a Saturday afternoon. But he relented, although driving along the Old Potchefstroom Road on a weekend afternoon is not advisable, especially between two and four o'clock in the afternoon. In addition to the normal heavy traffic, there is always a crowd headed for the hospital to visit the sick, not to mention the funeral processions going to Avalon Cemetery.

We were cruising along when the car in front stopped suddenly, almost knocking us off the road. Bra Thabo started to get out of his car to protest, but we realized that the terrible driver who had almost killed us had stopped to allow a funeral procession to enter the intersection ahead. With our tradition of respect for the dead, we only protested at the manner in which we had been stopped. We didn't particularly mind being stopped and accepted having to wait until the funeral had passed. After all, what other respect could we offer the dead?

One car after another went by as part of the procession. The cars were joined by vans and buses. The buses were full of boys and girls chanting freedom songs and waving their fists. The buses had no window panes and the children sat on the open frames. The girls' gym skirts billowed this way and that from the wind as the bus went by. It was very obvious that it was a student's funeral. People stood on the pavement watching the youngsters and looking out for the police and soldiers who usually accompany such an event.

"What bravery," I said.

"You call that bravery," asked Bra Thabo. "To me, it is the height of stupidity. Should one of those kids fall and break their neck, would that be an act of bravery?"

We began to argue. Perhaps we had been sitting in the car too long and the heat was making us irritable.

"You call that courage?" Bra Thabo asked again. "Look at what this fool ahead of us did. The correct thing would have been to ask a traffic officer to direct the procession. Failing to do that, they could at least have planted somebody to help with the traffic. No, instead, they force people off the road, almost causing accidents. Supposing I go and ask him what rubbish is this, will he stand for it?

"In fact, I think that is the trouble with us here in South Africa. We really do not have any respect for each other. That fool is probably feared where he comes from and thinks that everybody is frightened of him. And people like you talk of bravery!"

I suppose I had asked for it and I was getting it good and solid.

"Okay," I said, "but it's not as simple as that. The problems run much deeper. This is just one of the ways they manifest themselves."

"Stop being academic with me about our problems," said Bra Thabo. "Stop telling me about the manifestations and deep-rootedness of our problems when our society is going to the dogs. I find no reason for self-destruction. I find no reason for those kids with a future before them doing the things they do. Would you, at the tender age of fourteen, have hung out of a bus window and sung slogans? Would you? And we had it rough, you and me. I walked barefoot to school, often without breakfast, but I knew what I wanted from life. Do today's children have any ambitions or aspirations? You tell me."

"Maybe you're being too harsh on the children," I said. "Take it easy. Our children have seen what we never saw. They've been dying like flies at the hands of the law. Our children have seen institutionalized violence and it has inculcated a culture which says violence is the means of achievement. To maintain law and order, the government uses guns. They had to use guns to make us carry passes. They had to use guns to effect forced removals of millions of people. Since 1976, we have been surrounded by violence. What do you expect our children to be like? You are the first person to tell me that if you put someone in a kennel, he will behave like a dog. How else can our children behave under such circumstances?"

The procession was over and we continued on our way still arguing about the state of affairs and the general behavior of people. We were approaching Klipspruit when we saw a group of boys running towards the main road trying to stop us.

"I'm going to knock those kids down," Bra Thabo said.

"No, you can't," I protested.

"Look, I'm getting sick and tired of these children. My son does not go about hijacking people's cars. If he does, he should also be knocked down."

The boys meant business. Some were carrying bricks, others thick sticks. Bra Thabo had no choice but to stop. He got out and adjusted his trousers and belt.

"*Ja* (yes), what is it?" he asked.

"*Groot man* (big guy), we want to join our comrade's funeral at Avalon. We need your car," one boy said.

"Really! You have stopped me because you need my car. And you expect me to give it to you, just like that? And if I refuse?"

Here we go, I thought to myself. The kids will take the car from him forcibly. What would happen to me? Would I get a chance to get out and, supposing I didn't, would the kids drive me to the graveyard? I would be a sitting duck for the soldiers. What could I do?

"Well, we will be forced to take it from you," the boy said.

"Look here my boy, this is my car and I worked hard to buy it. If you think I am going to be threatened by you just like that, you are playing. There it is, my boys. And I am promising you one thing. Let any one get in there and drive off in my car and I'll show you a thing or two."

He gave them a contemptuous look. He was getting really worked up.

"You know, we are getting sick and tired of being bullied by you kids. Who says you can go about taking people's cars? Actually, who are you working for? Did Mandela tell you to do this? You nincompoops. If Mandela was released tomorrow, you would also hijack his car in the name of the struggle! Who the hell do you think you are fighting for, doing all these things? Are you liberating us by these actions? Anyway, I am not going to the funeral and neither is my car."

He looked at them as though he were going to spit into their faces and then got back into the car. I was shaking like a leaf. He adjusted his seat, looked into his rearview mirror, saw the coast was clear, started his car and, moving off, almost knocked down one of the boys. I thought they were going to stone the car, but they didn't.

LATER IN BED, I thought of all I had gone through that day and realized that such things were becoming our way of life. I wondered where it had all started and where it would end. Nine years ago, Soweto had been a beautiful place to live in. One only had to say Soweto and everyone listened. People in the homelands envied people from Johannesburg. Soweto, they said. People from other townships copied our styles and ways. We were trend setters. We were called names. We were South Africa. There were interesting and hair-raising tales about Soweto. Depending on one's lifestyle, Soweto was many things to many people.

I remember how at boarding school, the children from Johannesburg were always singled out as better, whatever that meant:

clever, arrogant, whatever. Once at school in Pretoria, I made the mistake of correcting a teacher's spelling of Orlando township. He took it very badly. "Only a child from Johannesburg could be so arrogant and point out my mistake," he said.

I lay in bed and thought of the Soweto I had grown up in. Originally, I came from Western Native Township which, after forced removals, was given to the Coloured population and is now known as Western Coloured Township. Western was a very small location where everyone knew everyone else. There was no Soweto then. There were a few townships such as Orlando, Pimville, Moroka and White City Jabavu. They were in the western part of Johannesburg. In the east, there was Sophiatown, Newclare and Western. Alexandra was on the northeast side of Johannesburg.

The South Western townships came into being gradually. As our rows and rows of identical four-roomed houses crowded the landscape, a people was born. At first, there were cultural clashes as the different communities met at stations, beerhalls, bioscopes [movie theaters] and football grounds. The Sophiatown people came with their American-influenced culture and imposed it on the more simple and down-to-earth Pimville and Orlando communities, who had retained their African ethos. With their Afrikaans lingo, they contemptuously dubbed the Orlando-Pimville people "turkeys." Gangsters flourished as the youth moved from one school to another. But in time, a distinct Sowetan culture was formed. By 1976, we were a diverse community within a single structure.

If there was a notorious gang operating in Soweto, one would soon hear of a similar but more ruthless one in another township. We developed our own bush telegraph making it easy for Sowetans to pick up the news and to know how to react to new situations. The bush telegraph helped us to be close. We cried together over various disasters, such as the Dube Bridge incident, the New Canada train crash and the Lourenco Marques (former name Maputo, the capital of Mozamibque) bus-outing accident. Sowetans came together to mourn their dead.

Soweto had been something to marvel at. Even at the height of discriminatory laws or when the most brutal gangs operated, Soweto remained dear to us. We laughed together and at each other and so improved ourselves. Even those who left to settle in the homelands, whether by choice or otherwise, never stopped boasting of their origins.

I lay there thinking of the different stages of our growth. I remembered sometime in 1976 when a group of students killed some thugs who had attacked their female teacher. Soweto reacted with shock to the incident. It had been normal practice for school boys to give chase to thugs molesting girls, but they had never killed before. We should have read that event as a warning that our children were no longer prepared to tolerate abuse.

Later, at a school in Naledi, a police van was set alight by a group of students. The incident was of such a dramatic nature that it left the police and people in a state of shock. In our world, where the law did as it pleased, it was something to witness children throwing caution to the wind and confronting the police. The police had become used to knocking on people's doors, demanding whomever they wanted, and leaving a trail of tears behind them.

On that particular morning, the police had gone to a high school in Naledi to detain a student. They were talking to the principal when the students turned their van upside down and set it alight. The look on the policemen's faces at seeing their van in flames and not knowing what to expect next was something to see. They sought a quick and quiet exit out of the school. The hunter had become the hunted as they ran out of the school looking for a taxi to take them to the nearest police station.

The incident made the headlines. It was the beginning of a "David versus Goliath" confrontation. But from that day onward, life in Soweto changed.

ON WEDNESDAY, 16 June 1976, Soweto was engulfed in pain, blood and smoke. Children saw other children die. They saw their parents shot. On 17 June, I watched as bodies were dragged out of what had been a shopping center on the Old Potch Road. I saw figures running out of the shop, some carrying goods. They ran across the veld like wild animals, dropping like bags as bullets hit them. I saw billows of smoke shoot up as white-owned vehicles burned. I thought the world had come to an end. I heard leaders inside and outside of Soweto plead for reason and I saw people detained and killed.

Unfortunately, we saw it all, adults and children. There was no way we could spare our children the horrors of the time. People came from all over the world to witness what was happening in our great city. We took them around, showed them the ruins, told them the youth were no longer prepared to endure the unjust system. We spoke of the youth who were prepared to die for a new South Africa.

Overnight, boys became men, and girls women, as they were detained, beaten to a pulp and killed. We watched the onslaught of violence against our children and were helpless. Children disappeared and reappeared in great numbers, as they sought to evade the authorities. We saw them address international conferences on the horrors in our land. At times, they appeared slipshod in their presentations, but they were very articulate when they described their pain and the kind of South Africa they wanted. We saw them leap over the stages of growth no human can leap over without incurring psychological damage. We looked on in silence, but at the same time we spoke of our brave children with pride.

The youth began to command control of everything. It was painful to be told we were no longer in control of our children. Perhaps we were not. We felt Soweto begin to disintegrate. The many threads which had bound us together weakened and snapped. Soweto lost its integral entity as townships and individuals began to distance themselves one from another. One township would be burning as another slept soundly. Some schools were in the thick of things while others continued as normal. Children were harassed by the police and parents made impotent by the law. Security police collected children in the dead of night and roughed them up in front of their terrified parents.

Children lost respect for the power parents used to wield over them. They realized that, if they were to survive the brutality of the times, they had to develop a new way of surviving. They had to become callous and lose their *ubuntu*. They were faced with a tough world where the game was always played according to the white man's rules. If the white man had to destroy to survive, to stave off whatever bleak future the black youth seemed to be orchestrating for him, he used violence to try and stop it. And the children learned to retaliate with violence.

Hopelessly we watched as day by day, year by year, life deteriorated around us. The exodus of students leaving the country mounted, as did the number of children in detention. Children had become an endangered species.

Nine years after 16 June 1976, violence was a blanket to be worn in the townships. There were locations entirely without teenagers. Many had fled to avoid the police, others had gone to look for schools elsewhere, a great many had joined the ranks of those in exile. Black mothers have paid a high price for giving birth to sons. In many cases, girls have suffered as much as boys.

At a recent meeting of students and parents, a woman who felt strongly opposed to the children boycotting school asked them what their plans were. "I am beginning not to understand your reasoning. The Boers are closing down schools and you are boycotting the very few that have not been shut. What is your story? After all, everybody knows that it is not in the interests of the Boers for you to get an education, so what are you aiming at?"

A youth stood up and replied, "We are also beginning not to believe that our mothers really suffer pains when delivering us into this world. You know that your children have been dying like flies at the hands of the soldiers. How many twelve-year-olds have been shot while walking in the streets? How many three-year-olds have been shot by police patrolling the townships? And what have you mothers done?

"Right now, the soldiers are camping in our schools, they escort us into the classrooms and to the toilets. We have to study under the barrel of a gun. And what do you mothers do?

"But if this had been happening to white kids, their mothers would have tucked up their skirts and fought alongside their children. How many more of us have to die before you join us?"

Ah, Soweto!

June, 1986

Schooling:
the Gathering Tragedy

TWENTY SCHOOLS HAVE already been officially closed and more
are surely to follow. It looks as though yet another year has been
wasted.

At the beginning of August, Soweto students called for a school
stayaway in protest of the presence of the South African Defence
Force in schools. Their demands included the release of detained
political prisoners and school colleagues hurled into jail during
the state of emergency. Until the government meets their demands,
they have decided to go to school for two days a week—Mon-
days and Tuesdays. The rest of the week, they loiter in the townships.

Last year, all seemed normal until September, when students
started calling for the postponement of the final-year examinations.
Most affected were final-year matric students. The government was
bent on going ahead with the examinations while militant students
threatened to assault whoever sat for the exams. The result? A
few students tried to write, but they were about to be lynched
by other students. They had to abandon the idea. Others sought
to write at some privately set up venues. But for most students,
a year had been wasted.

At the beginning of this year, there was mayhem as students
flocked back to school demanding, in some instances, to be pushed
to the next class. Using the slogan "an injury to one is an injury to all," schoolyard logic demanded "pass one, pass all." Some

had not seen the inside of a classroom for years. They wrote examinations sometime around Easter and, of course, demanded to be promoted.

As things stand in Soweto and most townships, schooling has long ceased to be an educational matter. It is political. Since 1976, when the students protested against the use of Afrikaans and thousands of people were killed, the education of the black child has moved away from the parents and educationists into the political arena.

The tragedy of this situation is that, in view of the prevailing political climate, the more fortunate black parents removed their children from trouble-torn schools and have either taken them to the homelands or to white schools. Those children left behind who wish to go to school cannot, and woe unto those who dare to go against "the will of the people."

The result is a new division in black society. Ordinary parents, for instance, feel great resentment towards those upper class politicos with children at posh schools in the Northern Suburbs. Then there are those "leaders" whose children study abroad while daddy stays home "fanning the fires of the struggle"—the same fires which keep the children of most township blacks illiterate and out of school. And *then* there are the activists who have been planning to call back children who are at boarding schools and at white schools. In fact, threats have been made to children attending white schools that their school combis will be set alight.

Another tragedy is that of Soweto itself. Its very size makes it uncontrollable. In some townships, life and school are relatively normal, while in other areas going to school has become a thing of the past. There is no way, for instance, a child can hope to attend school normally in townships like Diepkloof and Meadowlands—already aptly dubbed "Beirut." Added to that, communication between students of various townships is rather difficult. Recently a thirteen-year-old girl travelling by train to school was assaulted by "comrades" who asked her if she didn't know that it was meant to be a stayaway day.

THERE IS TALK of students calling for "People's Education." Proponents of this type of education claim black students are being taught distorted history and that the education fails to prepare the children for the adult world. To many South African parents, this is old hat. In fact, much was said and written about this when Bantu education was introduced in the 1950s. Came the 1976 black student uprisings and once again the inferiority of the black education system was under the spotlight.

So far, nobody has explained to the average black parent what "People's Education" really means. They need to know whether it is an ideology, a concept, a document or a syllabus. They want to know if today there is machinery ready to put it into action. They want to know if it is an alternative to the present system of education, or "brainwashing," or a gimmick, or a temporary tactic of a faction in the struggle, or if it indeed offers real hope. Presently there are three schools of thought vis-à-vis black education.

The first calls for "liberation now and education later." The second calls for "People's Education." Both of these schools seem to be aligned with existing political movements. The third school is the school of ordinary "non-political" people, who feel the black child is being made a sacrificial lamb.

Since the political movements are known to be active in all areas, why is it that it is only the Soweto child who is expected to boycott school. Schooling is normal in Eldorado and in Lenasia. What will happen when *uhuru* comes?

Black South Africans tend to want to draw a parallel with the Zimbabwe experience. Indeed, Zimbabwe is a shining example of what may be achieved. But, the Zimbabwe kids who became disenchanted with the old system went to the bush. When the battle was won, Mugabe was able to absorb the guerrillas into the army.

WHAT WILL HAPPEN to the black youth who has neither been to school nor to the bush. Who is even thinking about this Frankenstein monster, this typical Soweto teenager, who is presently ravaging the townships?

When Samora Machel won the war in Mozambique, he was faced by a nation where four out of every five members of the population were illiterate. One of his first priorities was to change that. In fact, the whole of Africa has been fighting against illiter-

35

acy. In South Africa, the black education gap was beginning to narrow. Never mind that for years people have been screaming that the education is inferior to that of the whites. The fact of the matter is, inferior as it is, the blacks who took advantage of it have not burnt their certificates and folded their arms in despair. Nor do we see them as generals of the "liberation-now-and-education-later" infantry.

Instead, they have carried their heads high and used black education as a launching pad to acquire more. We have them as doctors, lawyers and scientists—both inside and outside the country.

MEANWHILE, THE WAR rages on in the schools. Even if the government does not close the schools down, there is no way that students in Soweto will sit for the end-of-year examinations. And if they did, on what will they be tested? What can they have absorbed in their two-day school week? Another year has been lost. And, as the struggle continues, they are growing older. They have to be admitted to universities or find work. Where will the "pass one, pass all" tactic lead?

Unfortunately, the situation in Soweto is such that people live in fear. There is a strongly believed myth that the students are a faceless and leaderless mob, and nobody dares question their actions. The leader who survives these days is the one who endorses whatever the youth says, be it wrong or right. People have opted for popularity with the students, because opposing them is to invite being necklaced.

Another disturbing dimension is the quiet stand seen to be taken by the ANC as well as the PAC in this regard. The education delegation which met the ANC in Harare earlier this year reported that the ANC wants the students to go back to class. But it would seem that the message was not broadcast loudly enough.

PARENTS FEEL THERE ought to be a stronger call from the movement for the children to go back to school. The parents feel that somehow students are under the impression that the ANC condones their actions. They are of the opinion that if the ANC could condemn the non-schooling of kids, maybe the children would see the rationale behind schooling and just maybe go back to school.

But there is another argument advanced: there is no way the ANC could condemn non-schooling because children are in actual fact doing what the ANC is not doing—fighting the South African government. But those in touch with reality know that it is not possible for children throwing stones to bring down the government. They see these children as sitting ducks for the SADF troops.

So, if the students go back to class who will then fight the liberation war? And there lies the rub. Any well-meaning organization will not unnecessarily expose the wider society, let alone its youth, to danger. When a group of monkeys is attacked, the older monkeys form a laager around the young ones for the protection and preservation of their kind.

Everybody knows the value of education. And if it was in the nation's interest to withdraw children from school, parents would oblige. But it is national suicide to deny youth education.

September/October, 1986

Another Day in Soweto:
Diary of Troubled Times

TUESDAY NIGHT, 26 August: I was seated in my living room helping my fourteen-year-old daughter with her homework when the phone rang. It was my elder sister who lives in Rockville. I knew immediately that something was wrong, because she is not the type to phone for nothing. She is a very calm person by nature. In fact, she is the one who is always in control in my family when things go wrong.

I remember when my father died. I made a big scene, screaming and throwing myself on the floor. My brother held me and tried to calm me down. Nothing could help. As if possessed by spirits, I continued crying. Anyway, it was my sister Catherine who simply said, "Look, it's Monday today and the old man will only be buried on Saturday. Don't you think you had better save the energy for then?"

That did the trick. I sobered up. If this will help you understand her nature better, then I should also add that she is a nursing sister—tough. So when I heard her voice on the line I knew something had happened. One of my sisters? My brother perhaps? Or could it be the old girl (my eighty-year-old mother who hardly ever gets sick)? I held my breath.

"Carol, I don't know what is happening. We are hearing so much shooting and I believe people in White City are being evicted."

"What, why should they evict people at night?" was my first reaction.

My daughter closed her book and, with eyes about to fall out of their sockets, looked at me, obviously trying to follow the conversation. My sister told me that she had just returned from the street committee meeting where it was decided they should keep their lights on at both the front and back doors, and to respond to any neighbor blowing a whistle asking for help.

"There is so much shooting, I wonder if there will still be people alive tomorrow."

She thought it was about rents, which is a nightmare. If you pay, you can get the necklace. So nobody pays, but people are scared of being evicted, or of one day, when all this is over, having to pay months and months of back rent.

"There was also another problem: Two boys from my area have been stabbed to death. Apparently a gang went to a shebeen, held up the owner and got away with some cash. When they had to share the money, they quarrelled and one took out a knife and killed these two boys. Do you know what this means? The families that have lost their sons might want to burn this boy's home and the shebeen owner is not going to take kindly to what these boys did to him. Where will all this end? Is it fair that we should be dragged into this mess? I mean, I don't know the inside of a shebeen, but when houses burn I might just get dragged into it. Is it fair?"

I tried to pacify her and tell her that things would be all right, nothing was going to happen to her. But in my heart I was not sure, I wondered if I would speak to her again. We held on to the phone not saying anything. I could hear her breathing on the other end of the line. Finally, she hung up. In the meantime, shooting was continuing. I now had to attend to my girl, who had a barrage of questions.

"Will the soldiers come to Chiawello too?"

"Why do they have to shoot?"

"Are people resisting evictions?"

"How long are we going to stay without paying rent?"

"Does it make sense to you, Ma, that we should just stay without paying rent?"

"Why don't they release Mandela to sort out all this mess?"

I tried as best I could to reassure her that they were not likely to come to our township because our matter was being attended to. We had started boycotting the rent long before it was a national issue because of the unfair rate we are charged. I don't know whether I was convincing or not, since I also needed somebody to reassure me right then. But eventually we called it a night, and I continued my reading in bed.

It first sounded like a firecracker far away, but, strange enough so I could no longer concentrate on my book. I heard the noise again and this time I knew it wasn't any Guy Fawkes crackers, it was gunshots. I sat up and shut off the light. Then there were more gunshots.

I got out of bed and tiptoed into my living room to see what was going on. I peeped through the curtains and there was not a soul in sight. Then the dogs started barking. From all the yards, dogs barked and the sound of gunfire became deafening. I went into my other child's bedroom. She was sitting on her bed, eyes wide open. She asked, "What's going on here?" I could not answer her. I went into the bathroom and when I came out both my girls were standing in the passage. The younger one asked, "Are they here now, Ma?"

I shook my head. I saw lights go on in my neighbor's house. I went to the phone and dialed. As someone said "hello," there was a sound of gunshot. I dropped the receiver and ran to my bedroom. The girls said we should get under the bed, but my bed has a base so we couldn't. We huddled on my bed. How I wished there was a man in the house to protect us. I have always felt my bed was too big. But with two teenage girls and myself on it, it was like a cot. My little one held on to me, her heart pounding like a machine. We prayed with our eyes wide open, all of us at the same time. Sleep eventually overcame us.

Next day I knocked off early from work, planning to have an early night. I thought of getting sleeping tablets to knock me out, but settled for a bottle of wine instead. When I got home, I called my sister who informed me her neighbor's son had been found dead from bullet wounds. As I drew the curtains to get ready for bed, I saw a neighbor whom I have not seen for some time. I ran out of the house and we stood chatting about the night before.

Then, as we stood talking, we saw a group of about eight boys entering yards on our street. I suggested we stand and wait for them as opposed to them finding us in our homes. They told us that the Boers were coming to evict us, so we should keep our lights on and doors open front and back so those being chased by soldiers could take refuge. I went back into the house and told the girls that there might just be trouble that night.

We were having supper when the first shot went off. We ran to the living room to see if there were any police cars or youngsters about. The street was deserted. We went back to the kitchen but could only stare at the food. We moved to the living room and sat on the floor. It was getting very dark outside. We saw car lights moving on our street. I prayed that it would be a friend visiting us. But it wasn't. And we continued sitting in silence. Then a shot went off, followed by another, and another.

I started panicking. I needed someone to help us. I grabbed hold of the phone. I wanted to phone my brother to come and fetch us. But I realized there was no way he could drive past bullets and get here. I thought maybe phoning him and letting him know that we were in trouble would make me feel better. His line was engaged. Dare I scare my sister? I decided against it and suddenly wanted to speak to someone who wasn't caught up in the mess. I phoned a colleague, in the suburbs on the other side of town.

It was as though he had been waiting for my call. My voice could not come out. When it did, I told him there was lots of shooting and we were scared. He asked for all the details and ended by asking what was I going to do and what could he do. I screamed, "Nothing."

At that stage I was shaking like a leaf. I held the receiver out in the direction of the street so that he could hear the sounds of gunfire. He mumbled something I could not hear. I suddenly hung up while he was talking. I ran to my bedroom and changed into my pyjamas. My girls, realizing the state I was in, started giggling. I suspect it was a reaction. In their shocked state it was a relief to laugh at Mother making herself ridiculous. I knew they were equally frightened.

Then the phone rang. I started. I was too scared to walk to the living room where the phone was. I feared someone might see me walk in the passage and shoot me, so I crawled to the phone. Then my pyjamas caught on the carpet and I fell on my face. And the phone kept ringing while the girls laughed. Outside the shooting continued.

I reached the phone after many seconds, which felt like days. It was the friend I had called earlier. I told him not to worry and that I would phone him if and when I needed help. I hung up. I hoped he had got the message not to phone me. As I was about to crawl back to my bedroom, the phone rang again. "What is it?" I snapped. It was a friend from Cape Town. He wanted to know if we were safe. I told him there was trouble and he promised to pray for me and the kids. I thanked him and hung up. One of my girls told me to tell my friends not to phone us. Strangely enough, she had also crawled to where I was.

Shooting was still going on outside as we crawled back to the bedroom. It now sounded as though they were shooting on the next street. We stayed on my bedroom floor, holding each other's hands. My big girl suggested that we stand against the wall next to the window so that if anyone shot the windows the bullets wouldn't touch us. It sounded like a brilliant idea. I asked her where she got it from. She quoted the "A-Team." I gave up.

Dogs continued barking. Then we heard footsteps in the yard and something fall. I closed Bongi's mouth just before she could scream, and we waited. We discovered the next morning that it was a huge dog scavenging my refuse bin. We went on our knees like we do in church, prayed and slept.

WE WOKE UP to a normal day with newspaper headlines of trouble in Soweto. I could barely walk. Sharing a bed with two other people is most uncomfortable and, added to that, carrying tension for two nights had just about crippled me. I thought of phoning my boss to tell him that I could not make it, but realized if I stayed home I would probably have to deal with the soldiers.

Work was a form of escape, even if for only eleven hours. I dragged myself to the bus stop. In the taxi, everybody was talking about the shooting. Their personal experiences and some of their relatives' and friends' were recounted. One woman told how her aunt had slept on top of her son, hiding him from the soldiers. The narrator was very dramatic and had the taxi in stitches as she drew the picture of her big-bosomed aunt squashing the poor boy beneath her. We drove past many Casspirs...and ambulances.

One of my friends came to the office. She was livid with rage. "You know what my son has done? He has put us into trouble. The comrades came to tell him to join them. They did not find him and they left a strong message that he should join them or else they will set our home on fire. When he got back he refused to go. He said he was not prepared to be shot for nothing. Do you know what this means? They will burn our house because of him."

I tried to tell her, "What do you expect the child to do? He is afraid. Don't you understand?"

She didn't. "Look, I am also afraid, but he has to go. He is a sissy. He must just go. Otherwise we will all die."

In the afternoon my brother phoned to say our younger brother's wife had been mugged and was in bad shape. He offered to take me to see her. I asked my boss if I could knock off early as I was not feeling too good. Frankly, I did not have the heart to tell him where I was going. I just thought some things are better not told, especially as there was no logic in mugging a poor woman on her way to work. Mugging someone when the heat was on for so much more important matters. I mean, how does one explain that behavior?

I called home and told them I would be late as "uncle and I had to go somewhere." They told me to be careful. I assured them that I would not fall. Apparently they had been entertaining people with stories of how I fell over my pyjamas in my panic and that I may seem tough on the outside, but I was a paw-paw inside.

The weekend was uneventful. Come Monday and I started the day with a call from my friend whose son refused to join the comrades. Now the comrades want to burn her. She told me the comrades had once more come looking for her son and when she objected to their manner of approach they got angry and said they were going to necklace her. "Do you actually think they will do it?" she asked.

What could I say to that? How do I know the behavior of

people who necklace other people? Is there a pattern one could perhaps follow or read about to explain the thinking of such people? She was very worried. "I mean, all I am guilty of is asking these kids why did they have to be so rude when knocking on my door. They knocked as though we were harboring criminals. Knocking at every door and shining torches all over. Now I am to be necklaced."

I suggested that she should move in with me. "I have thought of that, but then they will think I am scared of them. No, I am not going anywhere. Let them do whatever they want." (So far nothing has happened to her. Knock on wood.)

In the meantime, there was mounting talk of the mass funeral to be held on Thursday. Rumor had it that everybody had to attend the funeral. In the meantime, the minister of law and order (What law? As for order, the less said, the better.) had already banned the funerals. We were heading once more for what might turn out to be a fatal confrontation.

THE NEXT DAY I was told there was talk about an indefinite stay-away from school, to go on until the troops leave the townships and release detained students. A friend called me to a meeting for parents to air their views. The meeting was attended mainly by women and students. The women were angry.

"I don't understand your logic," said one woman. "The Boers are closing down the schools and you are calling a boycott. In whose interest is all this? The Boers do not care a damn if you go to school or not and you are playing right into their hands."

The meeting got out of order as it became obvious that there was no way the children would listen. One of the students went on a long talk about how the parents have not taken any interest in their kids. "We have had enough. Try and read under the barrel of a gun. We are not wanting too much by wanting the SADF out of the schoolyards."

It was a hopeless situation. In one corner of the group, we (the mothers) admired those children and how determined they were. But we did not want liberation to be like this. The meeting went on with no more talk of the adults' concerns. The children called the tune and our only role was to sit and listen, in angry silence. It was not even as if they were a majority. They were a handful.

Wednesday found everybody worried about the next day (the day of the funeral). I knocked off early, anticipating transport problems. We had an early supper. Knowing we were not going to work the next day, we indulged in watching a movie on television. Around 10 P.M., a car stopped outside. We turned the lights off and peeped through the window. It was a friend. We let him in. He joined us, watched the movie, and the little girl soon retired to sleep. While watching we spoke about the funeral and what was likely to happen. I kept teasing him that as an ex-political prisoner he was meant to know what was going on. He told me that people of his generation were regarded as "has-beens" and the young radicals had taken over and "that lot does not listen to anybody's advice."

We were seated in that semi-darkness talking and watching the movie when suddenly dogs started barking. Soon there were whistles and voices. I stopped breathing for a second. I rushed to the window and looked through the curtains. A group of young boys and girls were throwing stones at my neighbor's house. I knew what it was. The next house would be mine. It was comrades collecting girls to attend the funeral vigil.

"Open up," I heard the youngsters call. At that stage I was shaking like a leaf. Then I saw shadows move towards my house. I collected my nerves and told my friend to open the kitchen door for them and ask them to wait while he wakes me up.

I remembered that a little while earlier we had bought a new cupboard. Bongi had given it one look and said, in what I thought was jest, "Now I know where I will hide when comrades come looking for me." I bet her she couldn't fit, and in fun she got in to prove her point.

That piece of childish fun was in my mind as I ran to my bedroom where Bongi was fast asleep. I rudely shook her, but she did not wake up. I couldn't carry her so I dragged her to the cupboard and locked her in. I then quickly took my dress off and threw my robe on as though I had just come out of bed. I met my friend at my bedroom door. He was accompanied by three boys.

The youths said they wanted my daughter. I looked them straight in the eyes and told them she was visiting my sister. I then walked past them to the door in a gesture to show them out. There were, I found, more youths in my yard. If they did not believe my story, they did not show it as they milled out. They moved to the next house where there is a teenage girl and boy. I went back into the house and ran to release Bongi before she suffocated. She walked half awake back to bed.

I peeped through the window and could see the youngsters moving into another house. Suddenly, I was gripped by another fear. What if they should decide to hijack my friend's car to the vigil? "I think you must go," I heard myself say.

He suddenly became furious. "Why do I have to be dictated to by children? I will go when I want to. Besides, I have the papers to my car so there is no way they can say my car is a target."

It took quite awhile to convince him that once they decided they wanted his car there was very little he could do to stop them. Besides, if they went away with the feeling that I was associating with people who refuse to transport them, then I might be in trouble. Having convinced him of the wisdom of leaving, I also asked him to take my daughter away with him in case they came back to search the house. Again, he didn't feel comfortable with the thought of leaving me alone. Ultimately, reason prevailed and we bundled Bongi into the car and they drove off.

Alone, I had a good opportunity to work myself into a state. I was now too scared to even go to my bedroom. I put all the lights out—comrades' orders or not—and took the scatter pillows and placed them on the floor.

I thought of phoning my brother and decided against it. What was the point of waking the poor chap, especially now that Bongi was away and safe? I dialed my boss. We spoke in low tones. There was no light in the house except for the two bars of the heater. He suggested I get sleeping tablets. I told him I had none. He said I should get brandy. We both chuckled because he knows I never get beyond wine. He sounded more worried than I. I was now sorry for having rung him. I asked him not to tell his wife until the morning, as there was no point in getting everybody worried.

I looked at my watch. It was only ten minutes to one. I thought of dawn. The creaking of the asbestos roof, something that happens every day, sounded like someone throwing things on the roof. I do not know when sleep overcame me, but I remember waking up feeling cold and stiff. Outside was a bright September morning. But already people were standing in groups outside yards looking at the main road where a contingent of army cars was moving towards Regina Mundi.

The day dragged on with all sorts of rumors circling the townships. There were not many cars moving about. I walked to the main road where I found one taxi fellow being told to unload passengers as no taxi was allowed to operate that day. People got off and started walking. One of them was a nurse coming from doing night duty in town.

Around Regina Mundi, a group of soldiers were standing in the church grounds while some were parked outside the yard. I noticed some more army trucks parked in the recreation park at Rockville. I met a colleague who was making rounds of the townships. I joined him in the car. We drove to the cemetery (Avalon) where we found soldiers guarding the main entrance. It was quite obvious there was not going to be any burial.

On our way home we noticed a group of people going round the back entrance. We had no doubt they meant to bury their dead. At that stage the army helicopters dominated the sky as they flew this way and that. We left the uncertain situation at the cemetery and went to the stadium. There was nobody there and the mood of the people around Soweto was angry. They could not understand why they were prevented from burying their dead. I went home.

Friday came and went without much happening. Everywhere people spoke of the high-handedness of the law. In the taxi to work people were talking about the rowdiness and uncontrollable state of the youth. One woman was agitated by the government for its refusal to release Mandela. "All what these children want to see is Mandela. I think he can put an end to all this tyranny."

Another was quick to say, "Why don't they just grab any old man and parade him before the kids as Mandela—the blighters don't know him after all."

The discussions centered around the youth and soldiers. Everybody wanted something to be done to redress the situation. Everybody was crying for security and a return to a normal life; a life where people can bury their dead peacefully, where children can go to school and not be intimidated by the presence of soldiers in their school premises, where neighbors can feel free with each other and where children can roam the streets as children, not as comrades.

I DON'T USUALLY wake up early on Saturday mornings. It was about 8:30 A.M. and I had just drunk my first cup of coffee. From my kitchen door I caught sight of a boy running towards me. He burst in through the kitchen door, ran into one of the bedrooms and tried to hide beneath the bed. I ran after him and ask, "What do you want?"

All the child could say was: "It's bad. The Boers are here."

He dove into the blankets, clothes and all. I told him how stupid it was of him to sleep with his clothes on. Who would believe him, whatever story he had. He got the message, undressed and threw his clothes at me. I locked them in the wardrobe and found some half-full bottles of old medicines and placed them on the floor next to the bed. All this happened in less than five minutes.

Outside I heard gumboot steps in the yard. I knew the soldiers were here looking for him. I quickly moved into the toilet. I heard them struggle with my kitchen door. One thing about my kitchen door is that it opens from outside. So you could be out there pushing when all you need to do is pull. No amount of complaining to the West Rand Board could persuade them to fix the door.

Ultimately, the soldiers got the door right. I heard them walk in the kitchen. I flushed the toilet and came out. Rifles were pointing at me. They seemed more surprised than I was. I don't know what they expected to see. It was quiet in the room. My cat crept closer to my feet as the soldiers walked to my living room, looked around, opened one bedroom door after another. I held my breath. They moved into the bedroom where my supposed patient was sleeping—and let him sleep.

Outside, more soldiers were scouting the area. Some were in the next yard and people stood outside watching. The ones in my house walked out. I started sweeping my yard so as to be in touch with what was going on outside. Having exhausted their search in my street, the soldiers moved on to the next one.

I gave the boy an old shirt that had been lying around for some time. After eating the sandwich I had prepared, he thanked me profusely. But there was no way I could not have saved that child. To me, it was not an issue for debate. It had nothing to do with principle or morality. He was a child who had to be hidden or killed. I didn't wait to ask him why he was involved or not involved. At the same time, I saw in my mind's eye a group of boys taking somebody's car. He could have been one of those who came for my daughter. He could have been one of those who are merciless when they want their way. He could have been one of those who wanted my sister's car or he could be one of those who petrol bomb houses. How was I to know? What would you have done?

I have seen a mother in grief. I have seen a mother coming out of Pretoria Maximum Prison after a visit to a son who was to hang the next day. I have seen a mother watching the corpse of her son covered in papers, waiting for the black maria to remove the body. I have seen a mother escorting a seven-year-old girl to hospital after the child had been raped by a man old enough to be her father. I have seen all that pain and I live with those memories I cannot erase.

Not so many months ago, a colleague asked me how I felt about necklaces. Proudly, I said they were the right treatment for sell-outs, all those people who collaborate with the system. I remember standing with one hand on my hip and carrying on about just how we blacks are weeding out all the bad elements retarding our struggle. He looked at me with a sad face, and I went on talking about soldiers killing three-year-olds playing in the yards. "Is it fair?" I asked. Why didn't the whites condemn that as much as they condemn necklaces. I was convinced we were on the right track.

ONE AFTERNOON THREE weeks later I was busy in my house typing away. My daughter burst in. I didn't like the look in her face. She stood there, her face losing color. I asked where her friend was. She told me she was at home. I went over and found her in bed. An irate mother said, "You know these kids can really make one mad. They go about the streets and look now, they are scared out of their wits. They have just seen a person being necklaced. If they had been at their homes they would not have witnessed such a terrible thing."

So that's what it was, I said to myself. I went back home, took my child in my arms and told her it would be over one day. We sat down and cried. I decided to go back to my typing but couldn't.

Something said I should go and see that necklace victim, but I was too scared. Eventually, the journalist in me got the better of me and I went out amid protests from my daughter. I made a few enquiries and people pointed the way the victim and mob went. A young boy ran past. His face had gone a strange grey color. I was about to turn back when I saw a group of people. Some were seated, others standing. I wanted to run back but realized that I might get into trouble and be asked why was I making a U-turn. I met some women in the way, talking in loud voices, condemning the killing.

"Poor child," one woman said.

"What did he do?" I asked.

They shrugged their shoulders and I went ahead. I didn't actually see the victim. His charred remains were by then covered in papers and pieces of plastic. But I saw the mother. She was crying, without tears coming out. If maybe you have seen a *sangoma* dance in a trance maybe you will begin to understand. She was crying and talking all the time. Maybe she was in a state of shock. But she was mumbling that her child was not a witch, but was sick. And she was crying to her God in Shangaan or Venda. She looked at us without seeing us. We looked at each other. There were women mostly (it was during the week) and a few policemen around. No one except the mother said anything. We just looked on.

People came, looked, got tired and left. It must have been sometime in the evening when the body was removed. Another victim of the struggle. Another day in Soweto.

November, 1986

The Matric Ball

IT'S 6:00 P.M. in a black township. People are returning home from work. As they drive along or walk from the stations, they stop to look at a girl of about sixteen standing in front of a gate carrying a banner reading, "My parents won't let me go to the matric ball." She stands there serenely and answers questions from passers-by. Occasionally, from the house, someone peeps through the window, smiles and shakes her head. It's her mother. Her father is busy working in the garden.

The lone picketer is then accosted by a youth who, upon reading the message on the placard, asks, "Say sister—what gives?"

"Well, you see I am a final matric student at Thaba-Jabula and we are having a completors' ball on Friday. My parents won't let me go. That is why I am standing here, registering my protest. I don't hope to get anything out of it, but I do hope it gnaws at their conscience, especially my father who is dead against me going out at night."

"You must be joking. Your folks refuse to allow you to go out to an innocent outing like that? What would they say if I took you to a shebeen? What they need is something more than a picket. Stay here, I'll be back soon."

The girl continues with her protest. By this time a group of people have gathered around her. And not too far away sounds of approaching boys chanting the current freedom theme can be heard. *"Siyayinyova Oh! Siyayinyova,"* they sing. They are led by the boy who earlier on was seen talking to the picketing girl. They are also waving banners with messages such as: "Down with irresponsible uncaring parents," "Release her or we'll burn your house," "Our parents are P.W. Bothas," "Away with tyranny."

They sing up to where the girl is standing. At that stage there is much commotion, as all the kids in the neighborhood have gathered around and joined the girl. Toddlers attending creche, teenagers at school, as well as the local vagrants have all joined the chorus, *"Siyayinyova Oh! Siyayinyova."*

Being rebellious by nature, the girl is quite amused by the turn of events until one of the boys threatens to open the gate. Suddenly the girl realizes what she has let herself in for. The smile of triumph that was fixed on her face vanishes as an idea strikes her, "What if they should set my home on fire?"

They continue singing *"Siyayinyova."* She begins to panic and runs to the boy she spoke to and begs, "Please stop, don't *nyova* it. Please stop. This is my home, these are my parents—please stop."

Regardless of her pleas, the crowds continue singing. They are now facing the house and threatening to bring the gate down. She runs backwards and forwards, shaking individuals and screaming, "Please stop." They simply push her aside and continue chanting.

On seeing the crowd getting wild and uncontrollable, her father drops the spade he's been using and runs into the house to confront his wife, "You see what your terrorist child has done? Now they are going to burn this house," and raises his hands up in frustration.

"No they won't if you allow her to go to the ball."

"Look, at this point, I don't care what she does, she can go to as many balls as she wants. I'm through with her," the father screams at his wife.

"Then you had better let her know that."

"But how can I tell her? I wouldn't like to be any nearer those mad murderous kids. They might just throw petrol on me and set me alight. What am I to do?" he cries, pacing the floor and cracking his knuckles.

Once more the girl's mother takes a peep outside and is petrified at what she sees. The children really mean to come into the house. She closes the curtain and storms at her husband. "Don't just stand there, do something. Get to Odesmeer [mispronunciation of Pollsmoor] or get Oliver Twist [mispronunciation of Oliver Tambo] to release the statement that she can go to the ball. Come on do it and do it fast."

Meanwhile one of her daughters who had also been part of the group had come back into the house and overheard the conversation between the parents. With a smile of triumph on her face, she stands between the dining room door and the kitchen and says, "Well, since I am also part of the protest, I am prepared to carry a written statement allowing my sister to go to the ball on condition the permission includes me also for next year, as well as all those other children who have the misfortune of having difficult parents like my sister and I have."

Now action and commotion is in the house and husband and wife run to and fro looking for a pen and paper to compose a statement to be dictated to their daughter. They both speak at the same time, saying the same thing using different words. Her concentration is disturbed by the noise coming from outside, while someone is heard to be warning and calling at the top of her voice, "*Nankamahippo.*" The daughter writes faster and faster as both parents speak to her simultaneously.

Finally she reads the message to the crowd waiting outside, "On behalf of all those children with difficult parents like us, in future you shall not have to go through the uncomfortable exercise of picketing your folks to attend school functions. You are given a blanket permission to go to wherever school duty calls until the casspirs and the law calls you to order."

"*Siyayinyova,*" they sing as they disperse, running away from the approaching hippos.

November, 1986

The Rocky Rise
of People's Power

IN THE CLOSING months of 1986, tens of thousands of ordinary township residents found themselves—unexpectedly, and usually for the first time in their lives—playing active roles in the political process. They have been caught up in the remarkable rise of the street committees.

From numerous townships, people report the same story. They were summoned to meetings, usually by teenagers and often on extremely short notice. A committee was elected, and since then they have, whether with enthusiasm or otherwise, recognized this committee as a form of local leadership.

This phenomenon emerged largely at the instance of the Civic Associations. In Soweto, where the current growth has been particularly rapid, it followed hard on the heels of the reopening of the Soweto Civic Association's offices after the return from detention of its senior staff.

The office remained the nerve center for only a couple of months. At the end of November its activities were disrupted by an action which may not be described (according to current legislation), but one of its key staffers happened to be absent at the time and another successfully passed himself off as a job-seeker. These two, currently of no fixed address, continue to further the spread of the committees.

What are the street committees all about? From Lusaka, the ANC has no doubts. They "grow out of the need of the people to defend themselves against State repression...and in response to ANC calls to make the country ungovernable and apartheid unworkable." So *Frontline* is told by spokesman Tom Sebina. "The main idea" is to forge them into "contingents that will be part of the process towards a total people's war."

In Pretoria, official comment is hard to come by. Off the record, security force sources display exactly the same perspective as Sebina. It's all part of the revolutionary plot, they say, directly traceable to the ANC's 1953 "M-plan," and is a development to be fought at all costs. This presumably explains why some 420 street committee members in East London, as well as an unknown number in Port Elizabeth (where the surge took place somewhat earlier than in the Transvaal), are no longer in active circulation.

In Johannesburg, in a cupboard-sized office which is normally the premises of a tiny trading company and is today serving also as the headquarters of the Soweto Civic Association, two men who spend their every evening instigating new committees laugh out loud, drawing a glower from the secretary who is trying to conduct the business of the company by telephone.

"The people in Lusaka can say what they like," says one, an amiable man of middle age. "We know that the purpose is to enable people to take their lives in hand. Local government has collapsed.

"The State's version of local government was corrupt and inefficient in any case, but local government is necessary for people to channel their grievances. The street committees fill the vacuum. They give people an avenue to express views and come up with solutions."

The SCA's plan is that between twenty and forty households should form a committee. The elected leaders of each street committee would represent their street in a block committee. Six or eight adjoining streets would form a block. The block committees would in turn elect the next tier of leaders to their township's "branch." Each of Soweto's twenty-six townships is to have a branch and the branches between them elect the fourth tier, which is the "interbranch." The interbranch, to consist of two members from each of the twenty-six townships, is to be accountable to the executive of the SCA.

Why this last step? Several different SCA people put the same point the same way. The interbranch, arrived at in this super-democratic fashion, is "accountable to" the executive of the SCA. This sounds like the tail wagging the dog. Surely it should be the other way around?

"It is necessary while we get going," says one of the SCA organizers. "We realize that the structures are unrepresentative at present. We are adapting these structures as the committee system builds up. Finally the leadership will come from the streets themselves, through direct responsibility to the people."

To this enquirer it still seems odd that the SCA executive should, even temporarily, expect some sort of supremacy over this 'ground-up' system. The organizer disputes this. "The government says the SCA is 'self-elected,' just as it said the Committee of Ten was 'self-elected.'

"In fact, the Committee of Ten was elected by means of widely representative organizations as fairly as it was possible to do at the time. But there was no mechanism for continued accountability to the people, so the Committee became the nucleus of the SCA, which has a fuller ground-level base.

"At the general meeting in '84, there were branches in seventeen townships. There were ten delegates from each branch, and the executive they elected included only two people who had been on the Committee of Ten—Dr. Motlana and Tom Manthata. Obviously, those branches were not thoroughly representative, but they were as representative as they could be at the time. It is not our fault that there were no elections in '85 and '86. Meetings were banned and many of our members detained.

"Now we are entering the third phase. The new structure will be far more representative, and it is much more difficult for the System to sabotage. Once it is fully established, it will be impossible for the System to put it out of action by detaining leaders. There will be a fully organized structure which can fill any gap."

How fully organized is it so far? SCA people duck the question repeatedly. They state vaguely that "many" street committees and block committees already exist. When pressed, they estimate that "about half" of Soweto is now organized, and excuse the vagueness on the grounds that their files have been confiscated.

It seems evident though that with or without files there is a very high level of uncertainty. The SCA people say that there are some freelance bands of youths acting in their name, but without any actual contact with them. But even aside from this factor, the SCA organizers have no clear idea of what their own efforts have amounted to.

Says one: "We know there is unacceptable behavior by some people who call themselves activists. We do not condone this but we recognize it as part and parcel of the kind of development we have to go through."

He gives an example: a shop was burned down "before it was established beyond a doubt that the owner was a collaborator." Does that imply that if his collaboration was established beyond a doubt, the SCA would condone the burning? "It is not up to us. The street committee and the block committee would decide."

Reception of the committees is extremely mixed. Tales of excitement are common. Many people have had experiences akin to the one described above. Some go further.

A Baragwanath nurse says that one direct effect of her committee has been to enlighten people to services they can draw from their neighbors. She has been introduced to a backyard greengrocer, and now buys her vegetables locally at greater convenience, lower cost, and with personal service. ("I wanted a pumpkin and they said you don't need a pumpkin today, your daughter already got one.")

A Zwide resident tells of the committee sorting out a problem regarding one man's troublesome dogs. He himself was reconciled with his wife after a twenty-six-year separation. The furniture movers refused to bring her goods into the township. The street committee inspanned the local comrades.

A Diepkloof man says: "It's wonderful to see. It's a revival of the old African tradition of the *indaba*—talking, and disagreeing, even angrily, instead of fighting. Ours stays right out of domestic matters. We don't go and beat up a guy who doesn't give his wife money. But we have put an end to the boys who used to threaten to beat you up if you didn't give them money. We all put in R20 a little while ago, and bought big pots which anyone can use who is having a party."

Generally, the positive comments relate to crime prevention:

• A woman in Mofolo: "Our committee is only two weeks old. Already I feel safer. There are patrols at night in case of crime."

• A man in Tladi: "We have had one for a couple of months. It is good. One man was caught stealing. He was sentenced to clean everybody's windows. We feel safer. Somebody cannot come to you and say he is a comrade so he can take your car. Now he has to go to the committee."

• A woman in Molapo: "Before, if your neighbor made a nuisance you could do nothing. Now you can take it to the committee."

However, there is another side to it. Take a selection of resident's comments:

• "Some boys I had never seen came and said, 'We are your democratic street committee which you have elected. The following are the decisions we have made on your behalf...'" (These decisions included instructions for bus and consumer boycotts, observance of days of mourning on 16 December and Christmas Day, and closing of shebeens and curfews at certain hours.)

• "If you work with the street committees you become tied to the UDF, whether you like it or not. I would like to have order and organization but I do not want anything to do with the UDF. The street committees become their puppets. They pretend to be democratic but they are there to carry out the UDF's instructions. The people get sucked in."

• "At first I was excited. I thought we were going to discuss the issues such as removing the rubbish that is strewn all over, and the electricity loan repayment that we make over and above the electricity bills. But these things are not touched. Instead you have the comrades running the show. I find it totally wrong for them to call us out of our houses to listen to them preach their ideology and tell us how they will deal with dissidents."

• "They make you take part even if you don't want to. One person who tried to stay out of it, they now have their meetings right in his house. To force people to be activists is wrong."

• "They are great for domestic problems and practical problems, but when it comes to political action there is no option. People who nobody ever elected to anything come to the chairman one night and say: 'The people have decided there will be a boycott. Your duty is to make sure that your street plays its part.'"

• "People who are not in tune with the UDF ideology are treated very shabbily."

Paradoxically, the very process of trying to develop order has so far led to a good deal of direct disorder. The SCA acknowledges various cases of committtee intimidation, ranging from several where youths called on householders to "pop out some monies," usually for "funeral fees," or knocked up adults late at night to berate them for failing to attend meetings, to one where a street committee pronounced a death sentence on an alleged sorcerer. (The sorcerer opened fire on his intending executioners, killing one teenager and seriously injuring another.)

Despite this, it is clear that in many areas a process is under way which has acquired a momentum of its own—the passing of power from ideologues to the hands of genuine community leaders.

In one case told to *Frontline*, adults revolted against the rule of a committee dominated by hard-line students and demanded a secret ballot in which everybody, including the youth, voted. To all-round surprise, a mainly adult committee was elected by such a margin that it was evident most of the youth had voted against their own earlier leaders.

In another committee, out of a street of forty-four houses (the precise figure is an outflow of the resultant organization), less than twenty people attended the first committee meeting. Many were there reluctantly, fearing retaliation if they did not attend, and many were particularly annoyed that they had been summoned by comrades at only fifteen minutes' notice. (The comrades apologized and explained this was for security reasons.) The meeting went well. Word got around. At the next meeting thirty-two households were represented, and this time people attended voluntarily, with no fear of reprisal for not attending.

WHAT HAPPENS NEXT? Do we have a huge clampdown? Does the ideological element triumph, with the committees turning into tyrannical instruments for imposing a "people's will" laid down from the upper echelons? Do we enjoy the unprecedented sight of true order, fair and full, entering township life?

In part, it depends on the government. At present the approach seems to be to hunt the committees down as just another step in the communist plot. This approach doesn't seem to have borne much fruit in the Eastern Cape, aside from maintaining full employment in the Prisons Department. Moreover, it has the ironic effect of aggravating the very polarization the government claims to be combatting.

One newly-elected committee member whose main interest is in doing all he can to make sure his child goes to school next year, describes this experience. "I was sitting in a committee meeting when three police cars came. I was so frightened I couldn't move. In fact they were coming for the house next door, where everyone has known for years there is a theft racket. Long after they had gone we were all still shaking. Afterwards I felt very strange. They could have been coming for me. I'm involved in fighting the system now."

It surely doesn't make sense from the government's point of view that a humble burger like this should find himself a "fighter against the system." If it left the committees in peace then it would remove much of the revolutionary ethos.

That too leads to problems. It is hard to envisage a time ever coming when the committee structure, no matter how stable and orderly and peaceable, would actively cooperate with the government in respect of civic administration. Whatever it might do in terms of establishing calm and control, it is surely going to represent a force for the end of white rule.

But there's going to be much the same amount of force to end white rule whether it comes from stones and necklaces or from elected leaders of coherent constituencies. The government's choice is not between pressure and no pressure, but between orderly pressure and chaotic pressure. Right now its options are to try to snuff out the committees and entrench the power of the paraffin artists, or to live with the committees and do what it can to strengthen the democratic strain within them in opposition to the manipulative strain to which they risk falling prey.

The Civic Associations too might do some constructive self-examination. For one thing, are they aiming to be political parties or are they aiming to be sheer structures, like town councils?

At the moment they are hybrids. They have no specific policy or program and they profess to seek primarily the generation of democratic order—allowing full and free debate rather than insisting on a party line. Yet they are affiliated with the UDF, and they have "affiliation forms" of their own for individual members.

Thus, if they are genuinely aiming at simply providing a structure for democratic activity, they are also unnecessarily inflaming the Azapo/UDF conflict and setting themselves apart from the rest of the community, which has no taste for playing a UDF game.

It's not easy for the SCA, with the police breathing down their necks at every turn, but nonetheless a good deal more strategic planning and public disclosure would seem to be in order. At the moment, the level of public disclosure is all but nil and, unless there are some remarkably convincing actors in the hierarchy, it would seem that private planning is not much higher.

They could for instance offer guidelines of legitimate and illegitimate committee action: methods of balloting, systems of linking smaller and larger committees, etc. At present most committees apparently consist of utterly inexperienced people finding their way entirely by feel. Many seem to have jammed at the point of rigging up community defense systems, and the flow of constructive example from those who have gone further—into mutual commercial support, for example—is limited to happenstance conversation.

The potential is enormous, but so are the dangers. The committees stand, for instance, to offer a thousand times better administration of small-time justice than does the existing combination of outsider (and often unavailable) policeman and outsider magistrate. But without a broader order around them they can easily descend to kangaroo courts. Above all, there is the ever-present prospect of thought-policing. Is the committee structure going to allow full voice to dissidents, even political dissidents—or is it to become a revolutionary Gestapo?

This question, like so many others, cannot be truly settled until the peculiar heat induced by minority rule has been done away with. But in the meantime, the torn and weary townships have hit upon the embryo of the only solution yet in sight to materially advance the quality of their lives. If the warlords of either side destroy the process for political aims, they'll have even more to answer for than they already do.

December, 1986

The Strange,
Strange Feeling
of Taking Control

THE SIGHT OF a group of boys calling house to house has become common. It is still unnerving. You think, "For whom does the bell toll?" When a group came up to my door and told me to attend a meeting the next night to form a street committee for my street, I was at first apprehensive. But the boys were polite.

I began to see an opportunity for me and my neighbors to organize ourselves so we would not be alone and at the mercy of the comrades. It seemed ironic that it was the comrades themselves who were inspiring this, but I started to get interested.

The meeting was to be held at a friend's place. I went to sound her out on the meeting. Apparently her house had been chosen because it had recently been enlarged. I found her terribly agitated. She could not understand why she should be picked on when she was a woman staying alone with her children. "There are so many men staying in this street, why is the meeting not held in a man's house?"

I told her that as far as I was concerned, that was not an issue to waste time on. What I thought important was the opportunity to get together as residents of that street, get to know each other, and, above all, to form strategies to solve our common problems.

I am not sure if she agreed with me or not, but, in any case, when the evening came, neighbors began to converge on her house one by one. At first people walked in, looked at each other suspiciously, greeted and sat down. It had been raining the whole week, so the night appeared to be blacker than it should have been, adding a sinister note to an already pregnant evening.

I really do not know what we were expecting. Of course, there were fears that the police might come in and detain the whole lot of us. Worse still, they could just get there and open fire. But then, so many people have died lately that one feels the presence of death all the time. And above that, we have heard stories about neighbors getting together in other townships and sorting out unruly events.

THE CONVENORS (COMRADES) arrived and were given suspicious and apprehensive looks. There were only three boys, none older than eighteen. They introduced themselves. I am not sure they used their real names.

As they stood addressing us, they shuffled their feet and rubbed their hands (I think they were nervous). They said the reason we needed to form a street committee was to protect ourselves, not only from the Boers who want to evict us from our houses, but also from the com-tsotsis (these are the thugs who masquerade as comrades). But, more than that, they said, they wanted to be together with us as parents.

Then the meeting was opened to the people. Like a pack of wolves, the parents descended on the three boys. "Where do you come from?"; "Where will you take our names to?"; "Where are your headquarters?"; "Do your parents know you are here?" were some of the questions asked, and all at the same time.

We were about to have a nasty confrontation, when one man spoke: "It's not as if you people do not know that street committees are being formed in most parts of Soweto. In this street we have had comrades coming here demanding that our children, girls especially, go to funeral vigils.

"The formation of a street committee is going to give us power to take what action we want to and not have them tell us adults what to do."

That did the trick. Some women were obviously still angry. Understandably, too. For there they were, face to face with people who were harassing them and making life impossible. It was obvious they had come along to give the boys a good telling-off and to say, "To hell with the street committee."

The boys were humble. First, they confessed they were not familiar with the jargon used at meetings, let alone conversant with procedures. Some women offered to open a night school for them. "Ma, we are boycotting schools." That derailed the meeting as questions such as, "What do you hope to be without education?" were thrown at the boys.

Someone realized that we were now off on a tangent and protested: "We are not here to discuss the school crisis." The people got back to the purpose of the meeting. Gradually, the ice began to thaw as the boys explained their stand and what we had to do. People asked for clarification on matters such as, "Does it mean that if you want to tell us anything you will go to our chairman, who will call a meeting and communicate to us your problem?" They agreed.

"Does this mean you won't come knocking at our door demanding our children?" The answer to that was: girls were no longer to be taken away at night. Parents heaved a sigh of relief.

The boys went on to explain how some elements were masquerading as comrades. The street committee would work closely with the comrades and fight all the unwanted elements.

They also told us no cars would be hijacked and Putco buses would no longer be stoned. "What is the point of stoning buses driven by our fathers? It is our parents who get killed and not the owners of the buses."

By this time, the parents were interested. We had also ceased to be on the receiving end—just there to receive orders from the boys. We were participating in the running of our affairs—something new to most of us.

Not only that. We had been gathered as strangers, who had lived next door to each other since 1982. Suddenly, we were no longer strangers and this feeling was to continue long after the meeting. In fact, we got to know each other better and better.

We then got down to the business of electing the executive. After a great argument, with people refusing to stand for elections, giving lame excuses such as "I knock off late from work," or, "I am already committed elsewhere," a man over fifty years old, who had made an impression with the common sense of his comments during the meeting, was chosen chairman. But not before telling the house that he was accepting on one condition: that he would never have to be told to necklace people or burn down anybody's house.

"I am saying so because our politics are no longer run democratically. If you disagree with the crowd, then you get necklaced. If I am called to do that, I want to tell you here and now that I will stop being chairman of this committee."

Once more, the comrades reassured him that they would not do any such thing. In fact, they said they were also against the necklaces and burnings. Our names were taken down, as were those of the executives. We were further told to buy a particular type of whistle, different from the ones used by the blackjack police.

These whistles are to be used when attacked by anybody, whether soldiers, blackjacks or thugs. The idea is to blow the whistle if attacked and, on hearing that, the neighbors come to your assistance. Unfortunately, recently in one area, people came out on hearing the sound of the whistle and were shot at.

The executive was also drawn from people who had contributed during the course of the meeting. One of them was a bus driver who had links with a soccer organization. It was obvious that his experience in running meetings for the team would be an asset for our street.

With the executive chosen and business out of the way, we spent some time chatting with the boys and getting to know them. The amount of good will created within a few minutes was amazing. The boys, whom we had viewed with suspicion and anger, had become midwives of security and understanding.

For days after that, I would meet some of my neighbors and we would actually stop and chat. In fact, last week, after four people had died in Phomolong, our chairman suggested we look beyond whistles for protection. We have now arranged an extra system of using telephones, which most people now have.

Not only that, last Saturday, a group of so-called comrades came demanding girls for a vigil. When they came knocking at my door, I told them that the issue had been dealt with at our meeting, that no girl from this street would be going to a funeral vigil.

I must have spent less than ten minutes arguing with them when I was joined by a group of women from my street who told the boys off. Previously, we would have been too scared.

December, 1986

The Deadly Duel
of the Wararas
and the Zim-Zims

A SATURDAY IN January. In an Azapo-held portion of "Deep" Soweto
there is a commotion. A group of people are chanting and wield-
ing firearms and weapons. Could this be a bunch of thugs or an
impi winding up the festive season?

On a closer look, one recognizes familiar faces. These are respectable men who clutch briefcases on Monday morning, rushing
about their business as insurance people, trade unionists and com-
puter programmers. They are conscientious husbands and fathers,
and I have listened with admiration to them holding forth at dip-
lomatic parties, speaking up for the black cause while clicking
champagne glasses and looking as if they had never touched a
dangerous weapon.

But this is the funeral of the mother of the general secretary
of Azapo, Mr. George Wauchope. She died of natural causes, but
politically related funerals have become battlegrounds for power.
The people are there staking out their territory and showing their
defiance of their rivals.

It is not like 1976. In those days the activists had their guard
up only against the police. Now, although there are many Casspirs
and Ford Sierras, and youths scuttle whenever the Yellow Mellow
armored police bus appears, the main conflict is between people
who used to be friends and allies.

In 1976 nearly all the activists were Black Consciousness, but
now some have followed one route and are with Azapo and oth-

ers have taken a different route into the UDF. The fight between the two is wreaking more devastation than the fight with the System.

Last year an Azapo member, Sipho Mngomezulu, was abducted from his home in Emdeni in full view of his helpless parents. His body was later found amongst the rubble in some veld. On the morning of his funeral, the family was getting ready for the burial and mourners had dispersed after the vigil, when some people set the coffin alight. Azapo members were alerted and arrived in time to stop the corpse from being burnt. Later, when the mourners were returning from the cemetery, a combi stopped and Martin Mohau (22), who was recently released from Robben Island, was kidnapped. His body was found at the government mortuary. From then on the feud has worsened.

Such is the life and death of people in certain areas of Soweto, Tembisa, Bekkersdal and portions of the Eastern Cape. In some cases, one group has had a member kidnapped and, to secure the release of their member, they would kidnap someone from the rival organization and an exchange of victims would take place.

While this is going on, life in the townships continues in a demoralized state. The school crisis, detentions and mugging in broad daylight are causing concern, and the rent boycott is a big worry as people expect lights and water to be cut off. That is the background against which the civil war of the townships takes place. Each group accuses the other. Azapo claims that the UDF wants to wipe it off the face of the political scene. UDF counters with claims that Azapo are the aggressors with the help of the police and the Makabasa.

"No," says Azapo, "it is the UDF who have the help of the police. Our members who have been found with weapons have been arrested but no UDF member has."

While the argument of "who's doing what to whom" rages on, people are dying. Azapo has the names of twenty-four people (sixteen in the Eastern Cape and eight in Johannesburg) who have died in the feud, in addition to many who have been injured. Now George Wauchope has twice had his home petrol bombed, and two of his relatives have died by violence.

What is it all about? Nobody is certain. Some trace the beginning to 1983 when the president of Azasm, Kabelo Lengane, was assaulted at Durban Westville campus and later at Turfloop by students who were turning away from the Black Consciousness line. Azasm—known as the Zim-Zims—remain in the Azapo fold, and have recently been chased out of some schools falling in the UDF area, but the same has applied to Sosco members in Azapo areas.

Some people say that the crunch came when Azapo picketed Senator Ted Kennedy's tour and forced him off a platform in Soweto. From that moment on, some Azapo members claim, the writing was on the wall. It was war. They say they opposed Kennedy because he was assuming the role of liberator, but UDF saw it as an attack on them.

Others say the conflict began as early as the 1982 commemoration service of 16 June. Traditionally, Azapo convened the main service at Regina Mundi, but that year, claims Azapo, the Wararas (a nickname for charterists, meaning people with no clear policy, the waar-waars) tried to take over. Azapo won the day but one of the speakers—Mr. Samson Ndou of the General Allied Workers Union—is alleged to have said that "those who do not recognize the Freedom Charter are not with the struggle."

There was also the fact that Azapo claims it tried to create a broad anti-government front when it inaugurated the National Forum at Hammanskraal in May 1983. It included people who were not Black Consciousness, but four months later the UDF was formed at Mitchell's Plain with the same objectives. UDF has since come up with numerous committees such as the Free Mandela Committee, the ECC and many more, while little is heard from the National Forum.

Other incidents also inflamed the conflict. Azapo sacked its president, Mr. Curtis Nkondo, for addressing multiracial gatherings and seeking the help of Mrs. Helen Suzman to secure the release of his detained brother. Azapo claimed he had acted against its principles by collaborating with government-created bodies. Some outside elements tried to put pressure on Azapo to reinstate Nkondo.

Then at the mass funeral at Uitenhage, Azapo members claimed that they had their T-shirts torn off their bodies, and the last straw was at that funeral when the UDF organizers allowed PFP speakers to address mourners, but refused to give Azapo a platform.

What is certain is that we now have a completely new kind of trouble. You feel the hostility between ANC and PAC as soon as you arrive, and if you land in the ANC camp then the PAC will certainly ostracize you and vice versa. You can innocently think that you are only calling on old friends who are now in exile, but you soon find that they have divided. If the first friend you call on has fallen into the ANC camp, then your next friend, who is PAC, will not even greet you.

But their war is a cold war. They do not kill each other. Even David Sibeko's death was finally attributed to internal PAC wrangles. First, there is no way the exile movements can start eliminating each other without earning the wrath of the host governments. Second, try and imagine any of the guys in exile being necklaced in Botswana or in London. It would create chaos. The bottom line is that it is in no one's interests.

But inside South Africa the organizations that are linked to the mother bodies abroad behave in a deadly fashion. This is also new. The split from the ANC by the PAC, when they were still in South Africa, was certainly not gentle, but at the same time it was not bloody. Now we have open war between forces, both of whom claim to be opposed to government. The war does not make any sense to many people, and leaders like Bishop Manas Buthelezi and Bishop Simeon Nkoane have tried to bring the groups together.

Azapo claims that the failure of these efforts is UDF's fault. Azapo president, Mr. Nkosi Molala, says that UDF people duck meetings or if they attend come up with "flimsy excuses" such as, "We need to get a mandate from our member organizations," and then do not return. "An issue in point is when we proposed that both organizations should tour the country jointly and instruct our supporters to cease fire. They agreed in principle but told us they would first have to get a mandate. They have since not come back."

It is not easy to get to the heart of the matter. What makes it worse is that in most cases these people have been friends. Some have been at school and university together, others have spent some time on Robben Island.

In fact, the situation can be very embarrassing for onlookers and non-activists. They have to declare loyalties that they do not feel and take stands that go against their principles. If you have a wedding you cannot freely invite friends, as could be done even three years ago. Now you must exclude supporters from either one side or the other.

So far, ordinary adults have not been coerced to join either side. Most people are not at all interested in either ideology, but only in liberation. They pay no attention to the war between the movements, except when there is fighting in their neighborhood.

Now every funeral of a young person is political football. One of the "Movements" will claim that person, even if he or she has had nothing to do with politics. An eight-year-old girl died in a car accident and Wararas went round collecting girls to attend the funeral. The Zim-Zims stayed away from this funeral. But funerals commonly end in more deaths and most people are frightened even to go to a funeral. What is more, both groups now carry guns, claiming that they are needed "for protection." In political deaths, people are not stabbed any longer. They are necklaced or gunned.

For youngsters it is more difficult to avoid taking sides. For example if there is a predominantly Zim-Zim school and the Wararas are chased out, then those who remain are seen as Zim-Zims. They cannot say, "I am not involved," because people will assume that they are at least Zim-Zim supporters, and then they can be attacked in their turn.

It is difficult to obtain comment from UDF sources. Many members are in hiding. One leading member refuses comment and threatens "consequences" if this story sees the light of day.

But Mrs. Albertina Sisulu, a UDF president, criticizes both organizations. She says: "Azapo must not pass the buck and tell a deliberate lie. It is not just UDF killing; everybody is killing. Azapo must not provoke people by running to the press and saying UDF is killing them. Both groups must come together and solve this problem."

February, 1987

Society:
Back to the Primus

COMING BACK FROM work I am suddenly struck by the unusual darkness of the township. It takes me back to the 1960s when there were few houses lit around Soweto, which led the American boxing coach Curtis Coke to say, "Walking through Soweto is like walking through a cemetery." Anyway, it is 1987 and although it is summer, in most cases by six o'clock some people have the TV sets on and some of the rooms are lit. This evening it's all dark except for the "Apollo" high mast lights on the street.

I get home and my daughter breaks the news—we have no lights and no water. Damn it! At the same time she produces my electricity bill that was delivered during the day. I must pay R114,00 or else my electricity will not be reconnected.

My mind stops functioning for a minute. So, I think, the hour has come. I look around my kitchen, almost every container has water. Apparently when the blackjacks (Council police) came dropping the notes, my neighbor, who keeps the keys to my house, opened my house and filled every conceivable container with water. I draw a chair and have a good gulp of water and my mind starts functioning once more. Do I have candles for the night? How do we cook?

Fortunately I still have leftover candles bought during the black Christmas boycott, when we had to light candles in solidarity with people in detention. But what do I do for cooking? I mean, it is fashionable to give away items such as gas stoves and primus stoves when we move up the economic ladder. We never seem to have contingency plans. Thank God it is summer and we don't need heaters and hot water. So the evening is spent using water sparingly and talking to neighbors about steps that need to be taken. People are worried about the food rotting in the fridges. Electric alarm clocks are not working—life is chaotic.

The next day round about noon I phone home to inquire about the water and electricity, I am told these have not been reconnected yet. It is January and mid month. I cannot afford a fancy gadget like a gas stove. I buy a primus stove.

Although I am of the primus stove generation, somehow I just feel I don't have to be taken back twenty years. With the fumes and noise it's like living in a hostel. But all the same, I suppose I should at least be grateful for small mercies, I could be in some homeland and be expected to make fire on the floor. By now, the water is in short supply. The toilet has not been flushing. To avoid problems, my daughter and I decide to go to the office and school toilets whenever possible, especially for bowel movements. We are only two at home. A neighbor has seven—what a mess. It is amazing how one can take things such as washing hands for granted. Washing hands before getting out of the toilet is second nature to many people. I must have turned to the tap a hundred times.

Each time after pumping the primus stove, I felt paraffin on my hands and I would rush to the tap. At the same time I couldn't take a cup from the cupboard and dip into the bucket for water, fearing that everything would smell of paraffin. I would have to buy gloves to wear when pumping the primus stove. The primus is another story. The damn thing makes so much noise you can hardly converse in the house. As for the paraffin fumes it exudes, I got a terrible headache because, it being summer with mosquitoes around, one dare not open the door at night. So we had to spend the night in a house full of paraffin smoke.

Not only that, one cannot regulate the stove's heat. It just goes full blast forever so you cannot produce any fancy stuff from it, not that one cares for that during the week but even good old-fashioned pap does not need strong heat. And, of course, my daughter would not go anywhere near it crying, "I don't know how to operate this contraption"—remember she is a child of the seventies when, even when there was no electricity, at least people used gas.

A primus means cooking one thing at a time. I cooked the pap first and ages later did the meat. By the time the meat was ready, the pap was cold. Vegetables were out of the question. And during the time I was cooking, I was dying for a "cuppa" tea. How spoilt can one get. One takes it for granted so much that while cooking you can have the kettle on and boil water for tea. I did not even have a kettle to put on the primus stove. I used a small pot for boiling water but the tea made from that water was poison.

My shebeen neighbors were the angriest of us all. Business came to a standstill. In fact, it was fun seeing guys trek to the next township in search of cold beers.

On the third day I ran out of candles. How does one run to a neighbor and borrow a candle on such days without appearing a fool? My daughter was beside herself with joy—I had for months been keeping a present of a fancy candle refusing that it be used. She brought it and I had no choice but to light it. It was a disaster. The light was not only faint but it flickered, throwing wax all over the show; so much for the prize. That night, she had pages and pages of homework and I told her most doctors and learned people she read about from black areas got their education under candlelight—some from remote areas lit a piece of reed.

We survived the night, as well as the weekend. We got the water back before the weekend, and I must say it was in a way great fun spending a weekend without noise coming from neighbors who own powerful music machines and who force people to share their terrible music. It was also interesting to see men not rushing to their next-door shebeen. Instead they would sort of saunter around the yard and complain about the mess the "comrades" have put them into.

ON SUNDAY A meeting is called. Everybody turns up. Nothing comes of the meeting, as it is obvious that not much thought has been given to the issues. Questions are asked and it is decided that a delegation be sent to the office to find out: (a) Why had the officials chosen to single out this township and punish it by cutting off such services? (b) How were the meters (especially the water meters) read, because there had been no clerks going about reading meter boxes in yards? (c) What criterion had been used on the electricity bills, as the amounts differed between R64 to R900?

The delegation came back a few days later with the news that the officials were not interested in their long story. All they wanted was for the tenants to pay; and they were prepared to accept payment in installments. The delegates then suggested that people start paying. Trouble began. The delegates were almost assaulted; they were not given a mandate to say that the people want to pay. In fact, until the whole rent issue is resolved the tenants are not prepared to pay.

THAT DIVIDED THE house. Some people felt they should compromise. They should not expect to get services free. Others felt that would be tantamount to giving in and they are not ready to do that, not while the rent issue in the Vaal, where it all started, still has not been resolved. Why does the government not deal with the Vaal first? Others felt that once Chiawello Extension 3 pays, then they will have let the whole of Soweto down. Then the next time Chiawello is in trouble, greater Soweto will not come to their aid.

Finally, the people agreed to refuse to pay. A few days later, I was surprised to find lights in the windows once again as I walked home. The electricity was back. I was pleased, but in a corner of my mind I wondered, "What next?"

The mood of the people is towards settlement. Some have come round with suggestions of opening a special savings account where money could be deposited for both rent and services. Their argument is: what happens to old people or those who fall under the low income group who do not have large sums of ready cash, when they are suddenly told to pay up? These are the type of people who might be the first victims of evictions. In the meantime, the comrades continue to talk very loudly about necklaces, and there is still much fear, even though actual cases of necklacing are now few and far between.

About two weeks later, the electricity was cut off again. The chairman of our street committee then visited the office. Finding no answers from the token black superintendents, he finally got through to an especially notorious white superintendent who said he should collect money from the residents to enable them to reconnect the electricity.

This, he was told, was to avoid letting the technicians come out to open up the power boxes for individual houses. It was much easier if it was done *en bloc*. People thought that was a reasonable offer. And it also proved that the superintendent was at least prepared to talk to the street committee through its representative.

Having collected the reconnection fee from each house, the chairman went to the office where he found that the superintendent had changed his mind. The superintendent would not take the money and instead told the chairman to tell the people to come and see him as individuals. He wanted to make them sign contracts binding them to pay the arrears. So one by one the people went and paid and we saw lights turning on first in one house, then in others. Despite our own anxiety to have our electricity back, many of us were angry to see people scabbing on the boycott. It goes against one's principles.

Also we thought we would see fires or petrol bombs at these houses soon, and maybe the appearance of the necklace. In fact only one person I know of has been necklaced for paying up, and so far only one house in my street has been petrol bombed. But the people who paid are still worried. They feel that their names have been noted. (Anyhow, the joke is on them, because now everybody's electricity is cut off again, whether you paid or not.)

When the comrades saw that the people were dividing, it seems that they felt they were losing control. They went with hacksaws to the power boxes and reconnected everybody. The whole street had been lit for three days when the superintendent got wind. Technicians came and switched off the main plant, once again cutting off everybody.

SO IT HAS gone on. The electricity has now been on and off so many times I cannot remember. It seems that each time, the length of time off gets longer and the length of time on gets shorter. As I write, we have been dark for three weeks without a break. As for water, that comes and goes too. We have learned to live with buckets prepared. If the water is off, it could be only a day or two. It makes life a mystery. When you come home at night you ask yourself "Will there be water or not?" Sometimes you find people washing clothes at night, a thing which was unknown before, in case there is no water in the morning.

What worries many of us is why we in Chiawello 3 are being picked on. In the meantime many other townships have also come in for the same treatment, but not as frequently as us. Is it because the comrades have a low profile in our area? Are we seen as "tame" people who crack easily?

The impasse is now bothering everybody. Each night one sleeps uncomfortably. People are now used to spending extra money on groceries, money which was meant to go to the rent. We don't feel better off, it is all just swallowed in the ever-rising costs. But we worry about how this is going to end. If ever we have to pay the arrears, it will kill people. Even just to resume monthly payments will be nearly impossible for many. But we know we cannot go on having house and services for nothing. No one is relaxed.

March, 1987

Why the Government Must Unban Black Political Organizations

FIFTEEN-YEAR-OLD Fana Mhlongo's body was discovered recently with a bullet between his eyes. Not so long ago, the father of activist Jefferson Lengene was kidnapped from his house and his body later discovered. A few weeks ago, Masabata Loate, a beauty queen who had served a five-year prison sentence for her political activities, was clubbed to death by a group of twenty-one young men. Four weeks prior to that, six youths had been abducted on their way from school. Three of the boys were later found killed and their bodies strewn in some part of Soweto. The list is endless. It includes Machoba of the South African Council of Churches (SACC) as well as many others.

Unfortunately the above macabre scenario is not confined to Soweto. In Port Elizabeth, for instance, we have heard of people being killed or disappearing. The same can be said of Uitenhage or Chesterville and Umlazi in Durban. In Soweto, things are so bad that some families have moved out and are renting flats in town. Each political group claims to be hounded by another and innocent relatives invariably get caught in the crossfire.

It is no longer a secret that a number of the deaths we have experienced in the black areas are political as well as ideological. The spiralling violence is made worse by the leaderless state the blacks find themselves in. Pointing a finger at the government and accusing it of creating the vacuum is to indulge in a luxury one can ill afford now.

Black areas are in flames. For sanity to prevail, there need only be leaders—people who are physically there for us to follow. And the only way of doing that now is for the government to unban political movements and let them operate openly and freely.

Until the emergence of street committees in certain areas, gangsterism in the cloak of "struggle" has been running the townships. That people have come round to forming committees is evidence of the need they feel to build a structure that gives them some control over the way their lives are run. Unless you are for a total collapse of society, you do not remove a structure without replacing it with another. For as long as the government continues to declare black political movements unlawful, gangsterism and anarchy will prevail.

Many acts of terror conducted in black areas are perpetrated in the name of "the struggle." If these organizations could operate above board, victims would be able to confront the leaders and seek an explanation. What do we have instead? Everybody and anybody who is callous enough to kill stands up as a leader. And soon we have an eye-for-an-eye syndrome. Stories carried by newspapers bear testimony to that. Somehow, there seems to be an amorphous group somewhere planning to put the fear of death in black people. Many people in black areas are asking questions as to who these people are and who they work for. For many ordinary people can still not understand how a girl like Masabata, who is reported to have served a jail sentence, could be brutally murdered while she had credentials of fighting the system that would shame most activists.

The hijacking of cars, targets and the non-schooling of children are issues that could be brought openly to the organization and direction be sought. For instance, people want to know if the issue being fought is Bantu education or education as a whole? If Bantu education is the issue, why then are some people against children who are at white schools? Are they not doing so to avoid Bantu education? Is this fact not clearly illustrated by some of the founding fathers whose children studied abroad or at prestigious institutions such as Waterford-Kamhlaba in Swaziland? Why is it then that the present child is seen to be denied the same opportunities? Does the organization want blacks to be perpetual drawers of water and hewers of wood, even after liberation?

That education needs to be brought to the level of every black man is not a debatable issue to most blacks. Most blacks want education to come down from the ivory towers to the level of every person. It should stop being only for the privileged few. People also want education to relate to society and its needs. But unless these issues are openly discussed and ideas tossed about, parents will forever be held ransom by inarticulate so-called student leaders.

For many years people have been asking the government to unban black political movements. For the sake of black survival the government needs to unban these organizations and so unmask the faceless man who put the fear of God into innocent people who want to lead their lives as quietly as possible. We cannot afford to let our people live in terror simply because certain individuals—who claim to be fighting for our liberation—would like to feel they can make the masses dance to whatever tune they call. The unbanning would give the movements a platform of openly coming out and condemning deeds of terror conducted in their name.

For years, blacks had the ANC as their only political organization. Even years after it was banned, people identified with it. Today most people find themselves antagonized by some of the things done to them and alienate themselves from any political movement. The bitterness emanating from harassment by people who claim to be in the so-called struggle can be measured by the violence and state of lawlessness experienced in the township. Almost all young people want to carry firearms. It is now a matter of kill or be killed, exploit or be exploited.

Those who have vision maintain that a leader is going to emerge from the present situation. Without the democratic structures, he will be as autocratic and dictatorial as ever and will continue suppressing opposition with violence. What will we have accomplished? We will have successfully removed a white tyranny and replaced it with a black one. Is that what we want? Unfortunately, the state of emergency as well as the clandestine way of dealing with our movements makes democratic thinking an unattainable goal.

If the government is really interested in the demise of black-on-black violence, then let the people's leaders come out and let us see what happens. After all, it can always ban them if they misbehave.

May, 1987

Elections

"I THOUGHT IT was your day off. What the hell are you doing here?" Madam asks of Judith, who is seated at the kitchen table slowly sipping coffee while listening to a broadcast of a soccer game.

"I decided to stay home and listen to the game," answers Judith without looking at her madam.

"Now you can tell me," asks Madam, "since when are you a soccer fan? Strange how you can swap your red mothers' union blouse for a soccer T-shirt," she laughs and gives Judith a pat on her shoulders. Judith looks at her and shakes her head.

"OK, Judith, cough it out—there's something wrong I know, what is it?" She pulls a chair and sits next to her. "Are you going to talk about it or sulk? Is it me? Is it master or is it the children? Tell me when last did you go and see your children in Soweto? How's your husband?" The questions come rolling out of her madam's mouth.

At the mention of her husband, Judith stands up abruptly and paces the floor.

"So, he's the problem—what's he up to this time?"

"He's stood up for elections," says Judith, still pacing the floor.

"What elections are you talking about?"

"The Soweto Urban Council."

"Oh! That's wonderful Judith. But why are you worried? Surely there's no need to worry. With his gift of the gab he's going to have a sweeping victory—come now, stop worrying. Very soon you'll be a councillor's wife—how nice. I can just imagine you in lovely clothes, smiling while being paraded to the masses. How sweet! Oh! my Judith."

"Stop it!" cries Judith. "You really surprise me. You mean to tell me that after all these years you still do not know me? You think that I could be impressed by being a councillor's wife—I, who have worked hard all my life, must now ruin it all by being part of something my people are dead against? Please Madam, please."

"Now Judith be honest with me now—what's wrong with being a councillor? Your people need to be led by their own people. We have our own councillors who enjoy our respect and love, except for a few whose names I wouldn't mention for obvious reasons. But I think it's only fair that you should choose your own leaders. Isn't it?"

"You see madam, the whole thing is just wrong. First and foremost, my husband does not even live in Soweto, as you know. He is a hostel inmate. How could he possibly represent people he doesn't know and doesn't stay with? The question which I need an answer for is how did he get himself in this mess, which in the end will drag everyone of us in."

Just then there is a knock on the front door and the madam runs to open it.

"Oh, it's you! *Jou skelem*—come in," and she smiles.

"Don't call me a *skelem*, I have never robbed or cheated you of anything," says Boy (Judith's last son) as he walks in.

"Just because you haven't had the chance yet. It's Boy, Judith, should we come over or should we sit in the lounge?"

"The kitchen is fine by me. Hi Ma! Pa is winning. I've come to fetch you so that you will be by his side when the results are announced," he says as he strolls to join his mother in the kitchen.

"Oh, my God. You've come to fetch me to be part of the circus. What has become of you my son? Can't you even try to show your father the way?"

"What do you mean Ma?"

Just then there is a knock at the front door. Again the madam rushes to go and answer the door.

"Oh, it's Po...Po...TLA. Damn it, I never know how to call your name. Come on in. You are looking very smart as usual, how are you?" She peeps outside before closing the door. "Oh! I can see you have bought a BMW now, isn't that something. It's wonderful I must say."

"Well thanks, it's the company car really. I couldn't afford running one. Where is Ma, is she fine?"

"Yes, she is fine, she is in the kitchen with Boy."

They walk to the kitchen. When Judith sees her son Potlako, she stands and rushes to his arms. "Oh, my son," she cries as they hug.

"Hello, Ma," Potlako responds and then turns to Boy. "And you, what puts you here, you want some money, eh?"

"No, my son, he has come to fetch me."

"Fetch you, why?"

"To be home when the election results are announced."

"Hey, come on, what elections are you talking about?"

"Oh! Potlako my son. What do you mean what election results? Haven't you heard? Where do you stay my son?"

Boy interrupts, "At airports and hotels—epitome of black middle class, running around in three piece suits and attaché cases..."

"Oh, cut it out. Each time we have an argument you criticize my lifestyle. Why don't you make up for your lousy lack of education by going to night school?"

"Me, going to school and become like you, you must be joking."

"Stop it you two," says Judith.

"And where do you come in? This is between brothers man'n," says Boy.

"Will somebody tell me about these elections, what's going on here?" asks Potlako.

"Your father has decided to stand for elections. He is representing Ward 3, which means if he wins he is the Mayor of Soweto."

"Heaven forbid. How can Father do that? He does not even stay in Soweto. And we can't even begin to discuss his leadership qualities."

"What's wrong with his leadership qualities? Because he hasn't been to university, that means he cannot be a leader?" asks Boy.

"Look here, that is not the point, the point is..." says Potlako.

"What is it? He is uneducated, eh? That is the problem with you people from universities. You look down upon everyone, even your own parents. Today you find so much wrong in father, as if you are perfect."

"It's obvious you've missed the whole point. Tell me, Ma, what are we going to do? We've got to do something. We just can't stand here and moan."

Boy insists, "Well I've come to fetch her. She has to be at home now."

Just then the bell rings, the master walks in and joins the rest in the kitchen.

"What's going on here? Why are the natives restless? Has the revolution begun?"

"You stop it Louis, we have a problem here. Judith's husband is standing for elections and he is winning," Madam says to her husband.

"What, you mean we are about to know very important people in Soweto? Friends in high places I tell you."

"And how," answers Boy.

"Well, I am going to open the spare shop I've always wanted in Soweto. Maybe a garage or two."

"Sure, sure, we'll see to that, I mean, Daddy and I." answers Boy.

"Now that makes sense. I've been wondering as to where you fit in all this, now I know," says Potlako, looking at Boy. "Why didn't you rather stand for elections instead of letting the old man do it?"

"Well, whether you like it or not, approve or not, I am going to help Daddy in this. I am going to drive the mayoral limousine, and I will accompany him to all the luncheons. Daddy and I will have a ball of a time."

"Don't forget to open my garages and spare parts shops."

"I wouldn't get carried away if I were you. Soweto people are no fools," says Potlako.

Boy looks at his watch. "It's almost five o'clock. Let's try and catch the news."

They all huddle around the radio while Boy tries to find the station. Soon the news comes on.

"The voting in Soweto went off quite well in spite of minor incidents of stone-throwing in a number of townships. The results are...Mr. Mabutho Xaba of Ward 7 won and he is the new mayor of Soweto."

"Thank God," screams Judith in jubilation.

"It can't be true," says Boy.

"I feel very sorry for you. It's a pity about the limousine. Better luck next time," Potlako says to Boy.

May, 1987

Conflict:
Mother of a Murderer

SUDDENLY LAST YEAR, at the height of "comrade mania," I heard
that the son of a friend of mine had killed a boy in his street.
The whole township was in a state of shock. Boys stabbing each
other are not unknown, but it seldom happens in our area. Occasionally people come back from the station with stab wounds,
but boys in the same street regard each other as brothers.

As I walked past the dead boy's home, I saw people streaming
in and out. The first place I had to go however was not there,
but to MaMokoena, the mother of the juvenile murderer.

At MaMokoena's house I knocked, but there was no reply. The
door was open, so I went in. MaMakoena was seated on her sofa,
wringing her fingers. We regarded each other in silence. At that
stage I didn't want to know what had happened. I knew she didn't
have the details. All she knew was what neighbors had told her—
that her son had stabbed the boy in the heat of the moment. After
a long silence, I heard her sigh, *"Ke pelegi eo"* (That is the price
of giving birth).

We made tea and sat trying to think of a way out of the mess.
The most direct problem facing MaMokoena was how to offer
her condolences to the bereaved family. She knew very well it
was important for her not to be seen trying to protect her son.

My immediate reaction was, since she was innocent, she should
be brave—face the family then and there and make her stand known.
We were about to get up and go, when we were saved by the

entry of yet another neighbor who blew her top when she heard what I had suggested. "How would you feel if your son had just been killed and you had to face the mother of the murderer? With tempers flaring as they are these days, the whole place will be in flames," she said.

As time crept on, a decision had to be made. We felt the best thing would be to gauge the mood of the township the following day. If it was not too hostile, she would ask a senior member of her family to accompany her to the dead boy's home. She asked me to go along too.

The next day, a child arrived at my home with a message from MaMokoena. She was ready to go. I arrived at her home to find her brother and sister-in-law there. Her brother, being a senior member of the family, would be her representative.

Walking to the bereaved home you could feel the tension mounting. People stared at us as we walked down the street. MaMokoena did not look to left or right—she had her gaze fixed to the ground before her, so as not to appear proud or defensive. Walking through the gate and down the garden path, the tension mounted. I realized that my being with MaMokoena made neighbors think I had taken sides. I brushed the thought aside.

Inside the house, we were confronted by the typical scene of a family struck by death. People were coming in and going out, prayers were being offered, followed by condolences. Earlier we had decided that MaMokoena would keep quiet and her brother would do the talking. After a hymn and a prayer, he stood up and solemnly offered his sympathies on behalf of his sister. He told the grieving family that his family would be more than helpful to the police in their investigations into the murder. This said, we had tea and cake, and left.

Back at MaMokoena's we discussed the state of affairs in our township. What was happening to our children, we asked each other. No one offered an answer. Ten years ago, boy stabbing boy was unheard of. Ten years ago, someone like MaMokoena would never have had to deal with such a difficult and sensitive situation as the one she suddenly found herself faced with. She was bewildered, shocked, hurt and angry that her own son could have committed such a heartless and cruel act.

What disturbed us all so much was the realization that we had problems with our children. While stabbings and killings used to be unheard of, they were becoming more and more frequent. In White City Jabavu, for instance, a girl had stabbed a boy to death not so long ago. Of course the students-cum-comrades had attacked the girl's home in retaliation. In Mapetla, a policeman had been necklaced by the local children.

So there we were at MaMokoena's, brought together by something so abhorrent and yet also so bewildering. What was happening to our children? MaMokoena knew there was no way she could leave the township. She would have to live with the hostile stares, she would have to face the consequences. Houses were so close together it was inevitable she would see the bereaved family in their yard.

"How long am I going to lock myself in this house?" she asked, despair contorting her face. "I didn't send my son to kill Oupa and if comrades are to set me alight, there is nothing stopping them from coming here. I cannot understand my son's actions. I mean it is bad enough that he has killed a person, but killing a neighbor...how am I to live with these people now?"

Having exhausted all the advice and comfort we could offer her, I left for my home. As she saw me to the gate and thanked me for my support she said: "I have gone over one hurdle. I still have to face the worst one when the body leaves for burial, all because of my son." What could I say, since that seems to be the curse of all women who have borne children. To me these curses all seem the same, differing only in degrees.

I remember the old days when at a wedding, as the bride and groom paraded the streets we would sing, "Oh la la, come out and see, ye childless women." Can we say that today as we raise our children with clenched teeth, hoping for the best?

July, 1987

Child and mother in a low income house in Soweto.

Shacks in Soweto with no inside plumbing.

The author and her son with her car in front of her house in Soweto.

The author, her son, and daughter.

The author's mother, a Zulu of the homeland of Venda. Mathiane's father was an officer in the Salvation Army.

A middleclass house in Soweto.

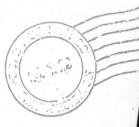

The author's daughter in front of the chest in which she hid when fearing an attack.

Young Soweto women at a lunch break in a Soweto field.

SATS Strike:
Working on the Railway

THE SATS STRIKE took a toll not only on the railway workers, but also on commuters. People died and trains were set alight. Most people stopped taking the trains; there was a scramble for buses and taxis. My station, which under normal circumstances is a hub of activity, was no different from a graveyard. The familiar faces of barrier attendants, booking clerks and laborers were missing. So were the pair of railway police constables who parade up and down the platforms, stern and vigilant in their immaculate uniforms. All of them had been replaced by soldiers with long faces carrying rifles.

I wanted to find some railway workers who would tell me their own stories, rather than the press statement material. Once it had been easy to do this sort of thing. People were keen to speak to reporters, even honored to have someone taking an interest. That is no longer the case. People are scared. You say you are a journalist, it's as if you have the plague.

One day there was a union meeting at Lekton House. I went down to Wanderers Street. Lo, it seemed like the whole of Africa was there. Hundreds of people milled in the street. Pedestrians, especially whites, were hurrying by nervously, thinking that something dramatic was about to happen. People were wondering aloud when the police were going to come. But in fact the strikers were quite harmless, just talking and waiting for someone to tell them what was happening, with the strike.

The lift was not working, there was a queue from the street moving up the stairs to the second floor, where the union, SARWHU, was temporarily housed, since Cosatu House had been bombed. (Lekton House is the headquarters of the "enemy," the black consciousness movement and its union allies. It was interesting, that in a crisis, the needs of the workers apparently rise above ideological disputes). I dared not approach the men in the street and ask questions. I had to get into the building and fish out one of the union leaders to introduce me to the workers.

I started the long climb up the stairs. Although this building is right in the center of Johannesburg, it happens not to be a modern building. The lifts are out of order much of the time and the steps are steep and narrow—and now they were sardine-packed with anxious, frustrated railwaymen. I wiggled my way up. Keeping my eyes on my bag and the ground, I elbowed and edged my way between the squashed-up throng. It was hot and the windows were closed. Sweat was dripping down my spine and legs. At one point, all movement stopped. We all stood stock-still for what seemed like an eternity, not knowing what had created the bottleneck. The smell of perspiration was frightening and tempers were running high as people screamed at the ones ahead to move on.

Although I was part of this hysterical situation, I was somehow removed. I was on another plane. Everyone was shouting for things to get moving, while I was paralyzed by other worries. Imagine the police coming and saying, "Three minutes to disperse." They could just as well say, "Take wings and fly," and in this place the tear gas would be murder.

That led to thoughts of a bomb going off. It had happened at Cosatu House only days before, and it could easily do so here. I suppose if I became a "journalist who died in the course of duty," I would get a big funeral and be some sort of martyr. But right then that thought was not exciting. All I wanted was to get out, but when it eventually became possible to move there was only one way to go, up.

Then I was on the second floor, which was also teeming with people. A queue marshall screened people on their needs. I extricated myself and kidnapped one of the leaders, who reluctantly agreed to introduce me to strikers. Despite his presence, the workers were not welcoming. Many gave us hostile looks, and we moved on without bringing up the subject.

Finally we found two guys who begrudgingly agreed to talk to me, on condition I was not to know their names. The unionist gave us an office and left us alone. It was like trying to squeeze water out of a stone. The guys were treading very carefully. I got the feeling that it was not only me they mistrusted, but that they were also each wary that the other might note down anything which might not be viewed in a positive light by their union. A few years ago, if you were speaking on sensitive issues, people would be similarly worried about things which might not endear them with the System.

THESE TWO GUYS were barrier attendants. During the strike they were living on the money they had saved, not starving like the laborers were. They spoke of terrible working conditions at SATS and said people were not workers but slaves. They were bitter and angry and the only weapon they thought right to solve their problem was the strike. They said the strike raised their level, and was now becoming a people's struggle for equality and dignity. They did not seem bothered that the strike was going on and on. They were sure that in the end they were going to win, and were proud of the union for leading them. But then, they spoke from a position of privilege; they had money stashed away in the bank.

I asked for details of the bad working conditions. They said one problem was the long working hours, but the bigger one was that the whites called them "kaffirs." I asked about wage problems, but they quickly glossed over that and returned to the matter of the whites' attitudes and being called kaffirs. They also complained about a "court" which deals with discipline at SATS. "At this court there are no blacks to listen to our point of view, only white people with an interpreter. They judge a worker and fine him according to their whims. We do not even know where that money goes to."

From these two I got the impression that 95 percent of what was troubling them was the way they were treated by white supervisors. To me this was an irony, because barrier attendants are known by everyone to have a terrible attitude towards commuters. I asked them why, if they were so upset because the whites were rude to them, didn't they stop being rude and churlish to the passengers? They didn't know what I was talking about.

Then I wanted their views on the people who had been found dead. Immediately, they started shouting at me. "What do you want to know from us? Have you been sent by the Boers? We do not know who killed those people and it has nothing to do with us."

I calmed them down by convincing them I was only interested in knowing the truth, and not in advancing the "line" of any side. After some time, they were able to rationalize the killings. They told me the people who had been killed were scabs. If scabs were left to do as they pleased, then there would be no end to the workers' problems. They gave me a long speech about the wrongs of some people who return to work when others are on strike.

IN THE TOWNSHIP later that day I met one of the barrier attendants who normally works at my station. He has a girlfriend in my neighborhood and had been frequenting her place during the strike. He was wearing his black serge uniform trousers, but not a jacket or SATS cap, which in the prestrike period he had worn all the time. In fact, barrier attendants live in their uniforms. I knew that he was one of those who had reapplied for his job and I was keen to hear his story. He was looking forward to the court case, coming up in a few days, which he hoped would bring about the end to the strike.

He said that as long as other workers were not back at their jobs, there was no way people like him could hope to work— "We are scared. But this boycott could go on forever. What will my children eat, how will I pay the school fees? For me it is even worse because I stay in a Railways house. If I lose the house, where will I stay?"

I almost told him he was not the only one, but I decided against doing so. After all, we all think our problems are worse than everyone else's. I tried to understand his case. He was from Giyani. Losing a job meant forfeiting accomodation. This would mean going to the homelands, it would mean his wife, who works in a factory in Johannesburg, would have to quit her job too or rent a room or move to the hostel. It also meant the children would have to leave the local school midyear and go to the homelands. They would have to acclimate themselves to a new lifestyle. He had my sympathies.

DURING THE STRIKE my street acquired new neighbors—soldiers. I came back from work one day to find that a hippo had parked three houses away, dropping off soldiers. What could they want? The registered tenant there is a docile Muslim guy whose only preoccupations in life are middle-aged women and fixing cars. Don't tell me they also think he is a commie.

The next day one of my neighbors disturbed my morning peace. "MaMathiane, do you know that short man is in trouble? Apparently he rented a room to a railway worker, one of those people who scabbed, and they caught him. Just before they could necklace him he escaped. I believe the hippos are here to watch the house in case they come for him. In the meantime do you know what he had done? He packed all his belongings and ran off to Venda. Now the poor short fellow has to live with the soldiers."

We had the soldiers for almost a month. We never knew what happened to them at night, but during the day, the white ones would sit on chairs outside the house while the black ones wandered around the street, going to the station and coming back with bread and all sorts of victuals. We got used to seeing casspirs loading and off-loading soldiers. The practice was soon dubbed "The Changing of the Guards."

The soldiers did not particularly intimidate anybody. On one occasion, when playing with one of the boys, they threw a stone at him and broke a neighbor's window. The neighbor stormed out like a cyclone. It was if she had been waiting for them to make one false move. She is a tiny thin-boned woman who you could blow over like blowing out a candle, but she tongue-lashed these fat, strong Boerboys with their fearsome guns on their shoulders, while they stood with tails between their legs. The whole street was in stitches.

Another person who was affected was one of the shebeen owners, who, when the soldiers discovered he was selling liquor, started frequenting his house. One day they demanded free liquor and when he refused they manhandled him. He simply stopped selling.

We woke up one day and the soldiers were gone, but the strike continued. Trains were being set alight, stories and rumors of deaths and assaults increased and a solution seemed as remote as ever. There were no railway workers at black stations. People boarded trains without tickets and paid in town. Soldiers were manning most stations. They stood in lines pointing their guns at trains, making us all feel nervous and irritated. One student remarked that, "They have moved from the school yards to the stations."

At New Canada, on several occasions soldiers threw tear gas canisters into moving trains, usually just as the trains pulled off. There would be pandemonium as people choked from tear gas. Such actions antagonized commuters who wanted to use the trains and brought them closer to the workers. They stood even more with the workers as they argued SATS was not only exploiting its workers but it was also giving the commuter a raw deal. Increased fares, unhealthy toilets and waiting rooms, and the strong possibility of being tear gassed made SATS very unpopular.

MONDAY 27 JULY, Midway station is once more pulsating with life. The men in brown overalls are busy doing maintenance work on the station, the barrier attendant's clipper keeps clicking. The gardener is preparing for spring as he prunes the shrubs and waters the flowers on the station.

But today is not an ordinary day. It is pay day and the first day after the four-month strike. One by one workers come back from the paymaster wearing smiles on their faces. The suffering of the protracted work boycott is paying off. A truck driver who earned R700 before the strike laughs aloud as he reads R1,150 reflected on his pay slip. There is jubilation, except among the scabs, who keep to themselves, not even showing their slips to anyone.

Having pocketed their pay slips, most of the laborers vanished from the face of the station. They, unlike the higher ranks, can leave for a special occasion without disrupting affairs. Next port of call is Lenasia, which happens to be the town nearest for cashing checks. Here they quickly get cash and move into the Lenasia hotel where they order expensive drinks—whiskey and beer. A rowdy, yet healthy, scene prevails as, with glasses bottoms up, the men look back at the past four months, a time when their jobs and lives hung in the balance.

One of the people to have been affected by the strike is the owner of the large tuck stop at the station. His shop sells everything from chewing gum to paraffin, from a box of matches to mielie meal. The back has been converted to a dining-cum-waiting room. He nearly closed down during the strike. With no workers and no one boarding trains, business came to a standstill, but his rent still had to be paid. Now he is slowly recovering. But today, everyone is at Lenz. "They will start drinking this [pointing to African beer] midmonth when their coffers run dry. For now it's whiskey all the way."

I spoke to a man of forty-seven. He joined SATS in 1981 as a laborer. Two years ago he was transferred from working on the tracks to becoming a gardener for one of the white supervisors. "I start work in the morning at 7:00 A.M. and knock off at 5:00 P.M. I look after my boss's garden, wash his van and feed his cats and dogs.

"I didn't get an increase like the rest of the men. I was one of many who didn't get it, although we were told we would get it this month. There was some problem with papers, and I'm sure it will start coming next month. Many people laughed all the way to the bank yesterday.

"On the subject of the strike, I am not very happy with the manner in which it was conducted. For instance, we were never formally told about it and the reasons for it. I heard about it through rumor. It was rumored at the compound that some Venda fellow had been fired and that the next day, it was to be 'tools down.' No trade union representative addressed us about it. Just then people died and it became obvious that going to work was not the best thing to do. I joined the strikers and attended meetings to hear for myself what the strike was all about.

"Personally I have no work problems with my boss. I hardly ever see him. He leaves his house around 9:00 A.M. and is back around 3:00 P.M. There is a separate servant working in the house. I realized that many of my colleagues did have problems after attending strike meetings and hearing what they were going through.

"I come from Pietersburg where I have a wife and two children. They are entirely dependent on me. My main concern was what would happen to my family if I lost my job. I am not young or educated, I cannot hop from one job to another. Who would want to employ a man as old as I am? So losing my job would mean my children would have to leave school and look for work. I used to sit at night and think about these things. I do not want my children to lead the life which I, as an uneducated man, have led. I do not for a moment enjoy living in a compound. I hate being away from my family but, to avoid exposing my wife to hunger and my children to a life without education, I have opted for life in the compounds.

"On the bright side, I got a lot of strength from my colleagues during the strike. As I sat at night agonizing alone on my bed, the next person would be doing the same thing. We were all not sure if it was the right thing to do and there were times when we would be on the verge of breaking, but come morning at the meetings, the leaders would revive our flagging spirits, telling us that victory was in sight.

"Some days we would see some of our colleagues who had not joined us receiving their pay slips, and we felt sore. We were starving and they were eating. Our children were going without food when their children ate. We felt bitter and hated them. Today, they are suffering and management does not know what to do with them. We refuse to associate with spineless dogs. Because of their scabbing the strike was prolonged. What hurts even more is that they knew that our fight was theirs as well.

"What I do not understand about scabs is that most of them were educated people who ought to know better than I, who am an illiterate. I am told they have big houses in the township and were afraid to lose them. We were also worried about losing our source of livelihood, yet we went ahead and downed tools.

"We know exactly who was working and who was not. Our colleagues used to patrol the railways dressed as ordinary commuters to see who was working. We do feel bitter about them.

It is not that there is violence, but we ostracize those people. If there is a squad travelling in a truck, we will not let the scabs ride with us.

"Many things have come right since the strike. Even the attitude of the Boers has changed. They no longer call us kaffirs and I saw the pay packets of many people yesterday. They received the promised increase. So what started at Gezina and appeared to be none of my business has worked out in everybody's favor."

July, 1987

Mahhala! Del Kevan

PASSING THROUGH MY living room, I noticed a white person being interviewed on one of the black TV channels. I was about to ignore what I was seeing when I heard, "People cannot expect to live in these houses for *mahhala*." I stopped right there and listened. There she was, Del Kevan, Soweto's chief housing officer—the woman whose name has been on the lips of a number of people in Soweto lately.

I had to sit down and listen carefully to what she was saying. She went on to say that if the people were not prepared to pay, they were going to be thrown out, as the backlog of people wanting houses was very high. She said services such as refuse removal and supply of electricity had to be paid for and that money was to come from the rent money. She went on, "There is nothing for *mahhala*. If you have any problems phone me," and she gave her number, which was beamed clearly on the screen.

I could not believe my eyes. Here was a woman, a mother perhaps, saying people would be thrown out into the streets. What kind of a woman was she? You can perhaps talk to a man about squatting, and unless you are an academic and bring in statistics, you are more likely to draw a shrug or some unintelligible sentence like, "What can we do? This problem is all over the world." But when you talk to a woman about being homeless, she immediately sees her own belongings thrown into the street, her children pulling her this way and that. No woman wants to go through that. And I want to believe that no woman would allow a fellow

109

human being to go through that. In fact, I am one who believes that a number of issues, left to women, would not have gotten out of hand, as has been the case with the rent boycotts in Soweto. In fact, I strongly believe that the tragedies of Wednesday, 16 June 1976 would not have occurred had the police force been composed of women. I could say the same thing probably for Sharpeville. But then that is another story.

I sat there immobilized in my chair wondering what kind of woman this was. I thought of the number of white women whom I know personally to be trying to challenge the wrongs emanating from the apartheid laws. I know many whose motives for doing so have been questioned but who, in spite of all that criticism and cynicism, have continued to build bridges, however weak, across the color line. I thought of a number of white women who have for years driven into black areas on charity work and tried to give fish to blacks. How often have they been condemned for not teaching blacks how to fish? I thought of the white woman who, after 1976, asked me what role I suggest she play to stave off the anger perpetrated by her tribe against mine. I remember feeling so sorry for her and telling my sister about the way she reminded me of Charles d'Arnay's mother in *A Tale of Two Cities*.

I could go on forever about what the white woman has done to empathize and to alleviate the burden brought about by the unjust laws of this land. I just could not understand how Del Kevan could be so heartless. We were talking about a whole community. Didn't we count for anything to her? What would she have done if she had been black and had tried to speak to authorities who would not listen? How often has one heard whites say at multiracial parties, "You know if I was black I would be in prison," and yet these very people are the first to call our leaders "terrorists." How many black journalists have had a tongue-lashing from white editors for calling freedom fighters "guerillas" instead of "terrorists"? What a place!

Anyway, there on the screen beamed Del Kevan's telephone number. I found myself reaching for my pen and pad and taking it down. After all, she had said those who need her help—I suppose those who want to pay rent and not be found out—could arrange a meeting with her.

In the taxi the next day, people spoke of nothing else but Del Kevan. "She thinks we will be intimidated by her," said one woman. "She says some people are paying, who is she lying to? Let them pay! I would rather be in the street than be necklaced."

One woman who claimed to be working for a large liquor store said, "I wouldn't worry by what that woman said. Who is she? I know her, she is a drunk. She runs a huge liquor store at work. She will soon be joining hobos in the park."

"I can't believe it," said someone else. "This is a dignified member of the PFP. You must be careful not to scandalize good *balungus*."

At that stage, one could not tell fact from fiction, a joke from a serious note. When I got to the office, I became even more interested in finding out what made Del Kevan so insensitive and arrogant. What kind of a fool was this? There was only one way to find out—I picked up the telephone receiver and dialed the number.

She was on the line immediately. Her husky voice said, "Del Kevan, yes?" I made a silent prayer to be calm. I knew if I lost my temper there would be chaos. I might very well end up in jail. I politely introduced myself and told her I had gotten her number from the television interview the night before.

"Yes, can I help you?"

"I hope you can. Mrs. Kevan, when you say people who don't want to pay rent will be thrown out in the street, what do you mean?" I asked.

"I mean just that. Are you one of those who want to stay in your house for *mahhala*?"

"Could you please tell me what is the meaning of *mahhala*?" I asked.

"It means nothing. Getting something for nothing."

"Really, nothing. Would you say my parents who have been living in Orlando since 1946, paying rent, but are now not, would you say *they* are staying there *mahhala*?" I asked.

"If they are not paying rent now they are staying *mahhala*."

"You mean the two months they have not paid rent is *mahhala*? I don't know what you are trying to do, but I can certainly tell you that it's not going to benefit anybody. What do you want us to do? Why don't you look at the reasons for boycotting rent and try and address them? Why do you people always seek confrontation rather than dialogue? Why don't you, for a change, listen to us instead of throwing us in the street and shooting at us? Does the power of the gun make you go mad? When will you ever start listening to us? What do you want us to do?"

"Why don't you people pay rent? Nobody will tell the comrades you have paid."

"That is not the point, Mrs. Kevan. How do you go against the people? Maybe you do not have insight into your own white people's history or maybe you have forgotten. But didn't the Afrikaners stand together to fight the British? Why do you want to divide us, and what makes you think you can divide us anyway?"

"Well, if that is the case, you will be divided out of the Soweto Council's homes. I have nothing against your struggle as long as you pay the rent, otherwise you will be in the street."

"Supposing I ask you to give me money to pay rent, will you?"

"I don't have money, I don't run a charity organization."

"If you don't have money, where do you think I get money from? We want to pay rent, but there is no work. What are we to do?"

"Well ask Tutu to give you the money, isn't it he who calls for sanctions? Go and ask him to give you work or money."

"Keep Tutu out of this! He has not evicted people from their homes, you have."

"Well I am only doing my job to the best of my ability. If you pay your rent you will have no problems, but if you don't then you will be out on the street."

"You know, when I picked up this phone to call you, I thought I would be able to penetrate your soul. I thought as a woman, I may just be able to reason with you. I now know you are beyond reach."

She must have detected the despair in my voice and it must have said something to her because she came back on the line saying, "You know I wish people could understand that I am merely doing my job. I really would appreciate it if people could pay their rent so we can get on with the job. And I must say I have great respect for you, because you are speaking to me decently and politely. You know some people have been calling me names on the phone. Some have actually threatened to kill me."

"Look, I don't know what to say to you myself and I think those who have threatened to kill do so out of desperation. I mean what can one really say to a person who is as insensitive as yourself?"

She continued to waffle and mumble something, but at that stage I no longer wanted to hear a word from her. I replaced the receiver and I wasn't sure if I had done the right thing by phoning her. I felt sure that I had wasted my time. Mrs. Kevan didn't impress me as even trying to understand the dilemma we were in. All she wanted was the black cow and its udders.

Ten days later, twenty-four people were killed by the Soweto Council police while resisting evictions and Soweto blamed her for each and every death on that fateful night. Three weeks later, a bomb went off at her house. She resigned her job, only to be succeeded by another white lady two months later.

August/September, 1987

Our Future:
Meanings of Freedom

SATURDAY MORNING IN the township. Suddenly the car ahead comes to a grinding stop. You slam on your brakes, and so does the person behind you. There is no movement. Tempers begin to flare. Motorists start hooting. On investigation, you discover that two taxi drivers travelling in opposite directions have decided to hold a conversation right in the middle of the road.

On such occasions, powerless and disgruntled motorists and taxi passengers throw their hands in the air and mutter, "What can we do, these chaps are a law unto themselves." It is at such incidents that one hears the remark, "So that is the freedom that black people are fighting for! The freedom to stop anywhere, and inconvenience anyone."

At the Zimbabwe independence celebrations, I was walking with a group of South Africans back to our various hotels from the stadium. Our hearts were heavy and we were all asking ourselves the obvious question: when was it going to be our turn? Then we came across a group of Zimbabweans seated on the pavement drinking Shibuku. They offered us some but we declined. One of them sauntered up to us, and with a drunken slur said, "We have long been liberated, freedom we have just had."

That statement hit me hard. I realized for the first time that freedom and liberation were two concepts whose meanings I barely understood. How much we were being bombarded with the two words and how everybody took them for granted. Recently I tried to find what they mean.

At a party I spoke to a woman who had been entertaining us about her problems with her colleagues, and how her blackness stopped her from being free and equal with them. She was on the ball and we were spellbound with her anecdotes. But then I asked her, "What is your perception of freedom? At what stage in your life will you say you are free?"

One would have thought I had said something terribly rude. She paused for a long time and when she spoke she said, "Freedom, what is freedom? I don't know." She tried to smile while groping for an answer, looking around at her friends for reassurance. That simple question messed up the laughter and the joking. People wanted to joke about how problems are because of our lack of finding freedom. What if we should acquire our freedom and then still have problems? That is not something to be thought of.

At a shebeen I asked some guys what they understood to be freedom. "The right for us to move into white areas and for poor whites to move into black areas," was one reply which got the approval of most.

Probing into the mechanics of arriving at that situation, I was told that perhaps not many blacks were financially qualified to go to white ares, but that many whites were sheltered by the privileges accrued by being white.

"As a whitey, you can get a loan to buy a house, a farm or start a business. The type of job you do puts you immediately in a good earning bracket and from there a number of privileges roll in. Whereas, if you are black, before you can qualify for a housing loan you have to meet certain obligations.

"There are many negating issues. So the government that we will put into power will have to cater to our needs as voters, or the struggle will continue," said one of the men.

Another said: "In the South African situation it means the whites relinquishing power to blacks." Another: "That we can do whatever work we are qualified for and live wherever we want to, like the whites."

The biggest argument was about whether poor whites should be brought to live in black areas. Some said there was no way whites could want to live in Soweto. Whether under Mandela or

Mlambo, ghettos will always be there for poor blacks, not for whites. Some pointed out that in Africa there were no poor areas where one could find poor blacks living door to door with whites. A classic example was Zimbabwe, where only blacks have moved up and not the other way round. "Have you heard of a single white who now lives in Rufaro township? They have kept to their lifestyles even if the standards may have dropped. Do you envisage a time when there will be whites who will live on pap and spinach? Even the liberals who are always telling of their love and empathy for blacks do not want to live with us."

Just as the thought of black freedom conjures up many ideas to whites, so it does to blacks. There seem to be two levels of freedom. There is the one level where people see Mandela, Sisulu and Mbeki back home and all the men and women in exile reunited in jollity. Beyond that is a curtain. People know there is something terribly wrong about the present system, but what shape a different one will take is something they cannot explain, at least not in words.

To some, freedom means the turning of the tables where the black man will be on top of the white man. There are many stories about what will happen when blacks take over. One woman maintains she will hunt down all the whites who were responsible for black suffering, lock them up at Voortrekkerhoogte and be their warder. On Sunday, her prisoners will go without shoes, winter or summer. Similar stories are common, half in jest and half serious.

Some see freedom as suddenly acquiring money and moving into white areas, while others see the disappearing of the police and casspirs in the township. To others the release of Mandela will be freedom. "As long as Mandela is in prison I will keep on fighting. I am not afraid to die. I have nothing to lose. But the day he is free, then I will be afraid to die," said an activist.

To others, Mandela's release means nothing. Nor does the scrapping of apartheid. "So what, we will still have to contend with staff reductions, price increases, retrenchment and all the constraints which black people have to live with." Whereas if the whole system is changed, including property relations and the abolition of large-scale private ownership, then we have a new order where the government will make employment available to the people, where people have the right to work and working ceases to be the privilege of a few.

For a domestic worker living in Jabavu, it is very different: "Things are getting better now. Even our wages have been improved, it is just that the cost of living has gone very high. If only the government can allow our children better education, I would say that we are free. Look, as blacks what can we do for ourselves? Without the white man and his ways we are useless. Lately the white man has gone a long way to improve things for us. I only wish blacks could stop killing each other."

"What is freedom?" asks Joe Khoza, who has spent sixteen of his fifty years on Robben Island. "We want to be free from oppression, but then what?"

He would like to see certain black attitudes change. "Freedom, to too many blacks, is the power to grab. To be able to get things. That to me is not freedom. Freedom is being responsible. It is the ability to keep time, to make an airplane fly and the lifts work. To be able to be honest with whatever duty is entrusted to one, and not to have whitey behind with the whip all the time to keep things moving." He further spoke of changing people's complacency. "So many black people know that their land was taken by whites, but have given up on themselves."

J. Cebekhulu of the Lembede Mda Foundation, which is based on self-reliance, maintains, "Freedom is the expression by the people of control of the land's resources." It is not the accumulation of wealth or education. For Mpho Mashinini of Operation Hunger, freedom is the right to participate in the governing bodies of the country from the grassroots level. "That is the one way which will ensure that everybody's interests are secured."

"Freedom is relative," says a Wits student. "What might be freedom for Dr. Motlana is certainly not freedom for my mother in Senaoane. Motlana is self-employed; he does not need to pander to whites and accept abuse from any white person. But my mother, who is a factory worker and is entirely dependent on whites, must swallow all they throw at her."

Writer Sej Motau feels strongly. "We know about flag freedom, where people suddenly find themselves free and don't know what to do. Some people equate independence with getting manna from heaven. What freedom actually means is the right to do certain things, allowance to do certain things. Freedom is more costly than oppression. Freedom has small print which people ought to read carefully."

To many, South Africa is seen as the last bastion of colonialism. Stories abound of how, in some parts of Africa, when the "natives" got independence they rushed into offices with pens behind their ears all wanting to be clerks. That does not seem to be a factor in South Africa. Many blacks have taken a look at what brought about the downfall of a number of independent African countries.

It may be true that some blacks think that come Uhuru then all will be hunky-dory, but there are many responsible down-to-earth people who only want jobs and education opportunities, and as one says: "laws made not by white people only, laws that will be made by us too."

There are some who expect these laws to mean changes in earnings. A nightwatchman says the present laws are double standards. "Look at my salary, I get peanuts. To me it really does not matter that I am uneducated. The fact of the matter is I watch over this building for fourteen hours and the owner is hardly ever here. But at the end of the month, he collects a huge check which he hasn't worked for and I go away with peanuts. Is it fair that he should steal from me by not paying me properly? He is protected by the laws made by his fellow men."

"I don't care for politics," said one typist. "All I know is the country is not run right. The whites are not happy, the blacks are also not happy. I do not even understand the freedom you are talking about because, if a black government takes over, there will be even more bloodshed. To me a black government is not the answer to our problems. We blacks need a person, be he black or white, who will put our case across in parliament. Someone whom we will vote in, not the stooges that the government gives us."

Her colleague did not agree. She strongly felt a black person has to represent the interest of blacks in parliament. "How can a white person represent us? What does he know about our plight?"

119

Although people had different ideas of freedom, they knew there was a lot they did not like about the system. Education featured top on the list of things they wanted to acquire. Housing and wages were also among the issues to be tackled if they were free. Voting came in also as a priority. The scrapping of the Mixed Marriages Act and debate about the Group Areas Act were non-issues to them.

But the more people I spoke to the more I realized how abstract a noun freedom was. If we had more understanding about what was at stake, perhaps there would be less fears, as well as less dreams.

August/September, 1987

The Emergency:
Waiting for the
Knock on the Door

ONE FRIDAY AFTERNOON in May of 1987 I walked into my office
and was told that the Soweto phones had been cut off again. A
friend, Thoko, was with me. She panicked immediately. "They will
be detaining people tonight. I spent four months in detention last
year, I am not prepared to go in again. I am not going home."

My head spun. My mind went quickly back to the last time
that phones were cut off. That was 16 June 1986. The state of
emergency had just been imposed, many people had been detained.
Everybody was anxious. As we were leaving work the previous
day, the 15th, someone said, "Chaps, I don't think there will still
be Soweto after tomorrow. The SADF is just going to drop a
bomb and wipe us all out." We laughed, as we South Africans
have grown accustomed to laughing off everything lest we go mad,
but we never knew when, or if, we were going to see each other
again. I promised to phone my colleagues to let them know I
was all right.

On the sixteenth of June, the sun rose as usual and I went
out to study the situation as we usually do on stayaways. My
neighbor was out sweeping her yard, and there were men congre-
gated in small groups looking towards the main road, from which
the army cars usually appear.

I wanted to know how my sister in Rockville was doing. I
went to the telephone and picked it up. It was dead. I hit the
bar like a mad person to get the dial tone, but the phone remained

dead. Incredible! I was up-to-date with my payments, what could be wrong? This had never happened before. Through the window I called my neighbor and asked her if her phone was working. She told me it was. I insisted that she check. She went into the house and came back with a look that told the story. It was not working. So that was it.

We spent the day in limbo, not knowing what was happening even in the next township let alone the rest of the country. The radio gave us only the usual news.

I have miserly relatives who phone me only on my birthday and on 16 June, or whenever there are new spates of stories about Soweto revolts. My mother is one of these, and I imagined the frustration she suffered down in Zululand, trying to reach her various children in Soweto. We survived the day seeing army cars going in and out of the locations. Occasionally one could see young people running away from the army vehicles, but generally it was quiet.

The next day, upon getting to work and once again being in communication with others, I was amazed at the anger the cutting off of the phones had evoked. People were saying things like, "Who do the Boers think they are to deny us the use of the telephones that we rent?" Somebody suggested that we take all the phones and dump them at the post office. Others wanted to know if we would be credited for the twenty-four hours that the phones were not working.

SO, WHILE THOKO was going on about booking into a hotel this May afternoon, I had been reliving 16 June 1986. My consciousness returned to the present to be aware that, in typical ignorant white fashion, my colleague wanted to know why they would pick Thoko up. Thoko explained that she had been involved in street committees last year. "Once they detain you, there is no guarantee they might not do so again." My colleague looked at me. I feared she might say something stupid such as, "But Nomavenda was also in a street committee, why isn't she being picked up?" This would just frighten Thoko even more.

Staying in a hotel was not the answer, alone in a strange place in town, unable even to phone through to Soweto. In Soweto, we can at least share our problems. I told Thoko that she should spend the night with me, where we could drive around and get to know what the Boers were getting at. She agreed and we set off for home.

MANY YEARS AGO when Thoko started teaching, I was already a journalist. I liked her but was terribly irritated by the simplicity of her thinking. She was neither apolitical nor unaware. She seemed content with the knowledge that she was black and underprivileged. She used to take me to task for being so outspoken. She would say, "We know all what you are talking about. Some of us are not talkers, we are action people, tell us what to do and then judge us from there." Did I have the answers? No.

In 1985 there was chaos in the country. People were being detained and others were being killed. Comrades and com-tsotsis emerged. Cars were forcefully taken away from owners, people were necklaced, houses were set alight, students were fighting among themselves, house rentals were boycotted. The councillors were evicting residents and, in turn, residents resisted evictions.

It was in that kind of climate that street committees were born. In some areas, street committees came into being as a natural process and at others they were initiated by comrades. In Thoko's area, it was the people who decided that their townships were going to the dogs and they needed to get together and fight the elements that were causing them sleepless nights. So they got together and formed street committees. Of course not everything was hunky-dory after that. But some semblance of order emerged. And soon the security police became interested.

Just before 16 June, they began round-ups. Thoko came to see me. She was on her way to the library. She said that one of the bigwigs in the UDF had called and said it seemed that they were taking everyone who was in street committees. He advised that she take to her heels as he was going to do so. I asked her what she was waiting for. She said that she first wanted to borrow a few books that she had long been meaning to read, and then she would go hibernate in some homeland. I told her she was playing games with the system. If word was out that they were coming for her then she had better run now or wait to face detention.

123

She promised to move out the next day. I told her this was a mistake. She said no, she was just a little fish and would be out well in time.

That night, she later told me, she woke up to torches all over and a knock on the door. She ran to her parents' bedroom and told them to tell the cops she was not around. Then she climbed into the ceiling.

Her parents went to the door. The cops asked for Thoko. Before her mother could answer, her father shouted, "Come out, Thoko, they want you. I do not harbor criminals in my house. If you have done nothing then come out and face these men." And as he was saying so, he was moving towards the trap door in the ceiling and the police were behind him.

You would think she would be angry with her father, but she told me that she actually laughed. "It was so typical of Papa," she said later, "he was such an honest person." She collected her washcloth and toothbrush and kissed her parents goodbye. Her father tried to inquire why they were taking her away and was told "routine questioning."

Thoko had spent four months in prison when one Saturday morning, after breakfast, she was told to get out of her cell. The chief warder told her she was being released. She was driven home in a van. She was not given any reasons for her release. On the way home, the van stopped in an open veld and the policeman told her she was being taken home but there was something they wanted her to do for them. She could live on easy street for the rest of her life if she would tell them of some of the things that go on in her township.

THOKO WAS FURIOUS. "I could not understand the logic of this man. I had spent four months in solitary confinement for doing nothing but being involved in street committees, which gave us the means to put our township in order. Now this man was asking me to inform for them. How stupid can some people be," she said. She then told him to take her back to her cell. But they proceeded to her home.

As she arrived at her street, she noticed people around her home. At first she thought maybe they had heard (which was unlikely) of her release. But as the van stopped she noticed the window panes were smeared with grey to indicate there was a funeral. Her immediate reaction was not to get out of the van. She didn't want to know who might be dead. She could not imagine her world without any of her sisters or brothers, let alone mother or father.

Jelly knees carried her into the house where she found friends and relatives from near and far. What was strange was the manner in which they regarded her. They greeted her as though she had come back from town or somewhere near. Not that she expected a hero's welcome, but the cold manner in which she was being treated was rather strange behavior. Her friends seemed to avoid meeting her eyes, nor were they warm towards her as someone they had not seen for a long time. "Something funny around here," she thought.

The kitchen was full of women. Some were peeling vegetables and others were cooking or taking food outside to be cooked by the men and women tending to the huge furnace specially designed for a large gathering. She pushed her way towards her parents' bedroom. There was her mom seated on the mattress amidst a group of women. A coffin lay beside them. Nobody had to tell her. It was her father after all. Thoko does not remember the rest, as women started wailing while some were busy reviving her.

Among her many friends present was Dimakatso Pooe. In fact, their relationship had long transcended that of mere friendship. They were sisters. Thoko is, in fact, Dimakatso's protégé. Having both grown up in Pimville and achieved certain goals, the two girls are looked up to by the community that is proud of them. And yet on that fateful Saturday, the usually garrulous Dimakatso seemed withdrawn and aloof. She went about the duties, serving tea and making mourners comfortable without mixing with the other women. I noticed this and thought it was because she was so close to the family; maybe the death of the old man was getting her down.

It was only when we were at the graveside that I began to get wind of what was actually going on. Apparently, some people had spread around the story that Dimakatso, together with Thoko's mom, had sold Thoko out. The reason, these people said, was to get at Thoko's father who adored her over all her other children. Well, that did not make sense to me. I could not for the love of anything think of any woman who could sell out her daughter. Secondly, I could not see Dimakatso ever selling out on anything or anyone. She was just not that type. I also could not understand the logic. How could Thoko's detention be used as a weapon to get even with her father?

I shuddered. At the time Dimakatso was riding on the crest of fame, being a member of the Soweto Parents Crisis Committee. It was quite obvious to me that there were certain personalities who felt jealous over her success and recognition. How many people have fallen victims of such slander and been necklaced? All we needed was some mad person to incite the people. I went cold.

At the graveyard, Thoko was in the dark. It was as we came back to the house that someone told her that Dimakatso was supposed to have betrayed her. I suppose they hoped that she would shun Dimakatso. In fact she went straight over and hugged her and they cried together. What a moving sight. Especially because everybody knew how false the rumor was. It had been intended to destroy Dimakatso. But in times of necklaces no one dared question people telling stories. It was another chapter of "For whom the bell tolls," and hope it never does for you.

Thoko's father had been stabbed by unknown people not far from his house as he was coming back from a funeral vigil in the next street. Early risers to work had stumbled upon the corpse on their way to the station and had alerted the police. In a way, her father's death was more painful to me than many I had heard of lately. It had become so common to bury people who had died from bullets, that his death did not make sense. To me it seemed incongruous that while we were building all sorts of protection structures against the governing system, this old man had to die at the hands of our children for no reason.

I actually felt the physical pain somewhere next to my ribcage as I listened to the sermon promising a better life than the one he had been leading. I was angry. We could not go on like this. How cheap could life be? What were we to tell our grandchildren? Psychologists were forever analyzing the situation and blaming it on the system. We had heard so much of that, and as a result we believed it was not our responsibility. How long would we continue to hide behind the veil of the system and exterminate each other?

I RETURN TO that day in May when I was taking Thoko to my house. As we drove into my yard my neighbor came up. She said: "Daisy [one of her daughters] was collected this morning for her involvement in street committees. They asked for you too, so you had better be ready."

At this, Thoko saw the funny side. Everyone was involved, so what was the point of hiding? In hysterics with laughter, she yelled at me, "You bitch, fancy saying I should come with you when you know very well that we were both in the same boat."

What else could we do but laugh and hope they do not come for us? They did not.

NOTE: When writing this piece I did not feel comfortable using people's real names. Many people suffered last year and many wounds have not yet healed. A lot of suspicion prevails and journalists face the arduous task of having to tread very carefully. Without real leadership our society has developed some unpleasant characteristics—namely finger-pointing and witch-hunting.

August/September, 1987

Violence:
Picnic in the Park

ON THE MORNING of Kruger Day—Saturday, 10 October—there were groups with picnic equipment waiting for taxis at arranged places around the township.

Now, Kruger Day was showing that a new era was on the way. It was the first public holiday of summer. The comrades had become a thing of the past. I recognized some of the people waiting for the taxis as ex-comrades. It was amusing to watch the same youngsters who only a few months back had put the fear of God into us so changed. For was it not last year at this time when they were knocking at our doors with all sorts of demands? Yes, people change and times change.

So, it was the first picnic of the year, but much more than that; once more our children were being children—going out and having fun. In the evening there was a great deal of excitement as the crowds returned. Many were chatting away, while many others were too drunk to know where they were. Such is the fun of today's youngsters.

On Sunday, stories of untoward behavior started making the rounds. Rumor had it that the kids who had gone to picnic in white areas had been disgustingly drunk, making absolute fools of themselves. Some had been admitted at Baragwanath Hospital where surgery had to be performed immediately.

Most people shrugged their shoulders. People do not like to hear these stories, but they are not surprised. We know it is a

129

fact that the kids will stab each other at picnics. What can one really expect when picnicking means the packing of liquor and weapons? It has become sort of a norm that when children go to picnics, some get hurt while others die; some may escape this time, but they may not next time. There is also the element of revenge which plays an important part.

It is not as if parents do not know that picnics are a great excuse for getting far away, well stocked with liquor and food and equally well protected with arms "just in case." Moreover with the white parks now accepting blacks there is always the chance that one township gang will unintentionally bump into a rival group which has chosen the same spot.

Besides, blacks are more at home in some places than in others, and there are some customs which people have grown used to. The Wilds is where wedding parties go to take photographs and where old people take walks and relax. Parents who want to combine a peaceful time with some education for their children make their way to Pretoria Zoo. Wemmer Pan, Zoo Lake and Lion Park are the places you go if you want noise and dancing and are not too worried about the risk of violence breaking out.

One wonders why the kids prefer to go to white spots when there are ever so many parks in Soweto. The answer is simple, they are not parks but death traps. How many times have early risers stumbled onto corpses lying at Thokoza Park in Rockville or at Mofolo Park. Mofolo Park is famous for people washing their cars and for secret lovers committing adultery in locked cars under the trees. For respectable people it is unthinkable that you could go to Mofolo or Thokoza and have a picnic with your children. It does not even cross your mind. People do not see these places as parks in the same way that they see Zoo Lake and the other real parks in town. Mofolo and Thokoza are just open spaces with trees, and thoroughfares between townships.

As for Oppenheimer Park—that has never been seen as part of Soweto. It has always been for the white tourists to end their trip of Soweto by looking down at us from the tower. After 1976, the West Rand Board blundered even more by giving part of it over to Credo Mutwa to create a *khaya* museum of sorts. This is for whites on the bus tours to visit. Local residents do not even know that the park exists. They see the tower, and they believe that it is a soldiers' memorial of some sort. After living in Soweto my whole life, I only discovered this park in 1980 when I was taken there by whites who were showing a foreign visitor around.

The rest of the parks are mainly used as thoroughfares. Few have any trees or grass, let alone water. A year or two ago the comrades had their famous campaign to clean up the townships. I must say that they did put in a good effort. We ended up with lots of clean spaces where there had been nothing but dumps before.

This presented its own problems. People were forced to provide money for paint. We suspected that the money did not all go towards paint, but those were the days when we dared not question. Anyhow, we did see that there was much use for the paint. A big stone or boulder would be painted yellow or black and there would be a sign saying "Welcome to Zoro Park—do not walk here" or something like that.

Whatever the problems, there is no doubt that the empty spaces were cleaned up. Now, however, they are filthy dumps once again. But even when clean, they were never really parks. So there is no local park for picnics. Even if there was, Soweto is so depressing, with the same sights of rows and rows of identical houses and identical combi taxis and identical Putco buses day after day, that people would still want to get a breath of fresh air elsewhere. They would still go to the white parks even if the government built a complete new Zoo Lake in Soweto.

It should be remembered that not all black children subscribe to the picnic world. There are those who are into soccer, youth clubs, putting on plays, or going to musical festivals. Of these, the youth-club set is by far the most peaceful. These kids are respectful and education-oriented, and anybody who touches any liquor, even a glass of beer, is frowned upon. The type that goes to musicals is basically nonviolent and rarely carries any form of weapon. Also, the festivals will show a good range in generation, from teenager to middle-aged. There can be fistfights, especially if liquor flows, but seldom more than that. The soccer crowd is also mainly harmless. It is in the picnic set that the violence is great. Boys can be strolling about as friends at noon, and by evening one or two can be at the mortuary.

131

ON MONDAY MORNING I was shocked to see the white papers—
the *Citizen* and the Afrikaans paper *Beeld*. They had huge reports
about blacks going on the rampage. It was like the report of a
war starting. There were moving pictures of white people bleeding
and their sad stories. But I also knew for a fact that there were
black people who had died and no mention was made of them
in the papers. Was that not news worth mentioning? Or was this
the objectivity the liberal press keeps talking about?

What actually happened? I thought the *Sowetan* would throw
some light on the matter. I searched in vain: The *Sowetan* did
not even mention it.

I went to Zondi township where I had been told there were
victims. I found a friend who stays in the area and we set out
to try to find out what had happened. Most people did not want
to talk about the drunken boys who went to town and started killing each other. "They had no business to go to the picnic drunk
as they were," said one parent. Another person blamed it on some
Portuguese guys who were selling liquor at the park. "What did
they expect. Of course they went there to make the people get
drunk. What did they want to happen?"

Most people knew nothing about whites being killed. Only a
few had seen it in the white newspapers. It was not a talking
point. The talking point was that black kids had gone all the way
to town to kill each other. That was something new. And people were sorrowful that there was trouble again. We know that
things will never be truly normal. We will always fear the next
uprising, and wonder what form it will take. But we had a short
glimpse of a semblance of normality that Saturday. We had been
secretly hoping for the best, and now it had gone wrong.

Some people put the blame squarely on the police. "The children were drunk and waiting for their transport when the police
came and opened tear gas. You know how our children don't want
to see the sight of the police. They went mad. The police pro-
voked the kids as usual. If they had left the kids alone, their transport would have eventually come for them and taken them home
instead of wandering the streets of Johannesburg and slashing people's throats," said one.

One thing I know is the effect police have over black youth.

If the police have guns, then they get even wilder. In their dealings with the cops, they have come to know the exact number of bullets police guns carry. And as the police shoot they are ducking and counting. Once they know the last shot has been fired they advance. So it is quite often unwise to bring in the cops.

I could also understand the adverse role played by the white guys who came selling beers. The kids had taken enough drink to the park already. What the white guys had actually done was to exacerbate the situation by replenishing them. Under normal circumstances, one would argue they were providing a service, but we don't need that type of a service. But how do they get the right to stand there right in front of a park and peddle liquor, a mobile bottle store? Can anybody do that in a black area? No way!

If the bootleggers had not been there, the kids would have run out of stock, slept, woken up babbelaased, and gone home. But now you had them demanding more, with no money to pay. The white bootleggers panicked and asked for the only help they can rely on to deal with blacks—the law. Unfortunately the police have over the years proved to be incapable of handling skirmishes of this nature. In many cases they have made mountains out of mole hills.

But, if you have seen children at work, you will understand why the Portuguese panicked. I have seen a Greek shop swept clean by schoolkids on an excursion. As they enter the shop, the girls flock to the counter and confuse the person at the counter. This is probably in some country town—you cannot try this trick with Harry Sam! The shopkeeper is confused, seeing so many customers. While he is attending to the girls screaming for this and that, he is unaware that the boys in the background are removing bags of oranges and crates of soft drinks. One told me how he stole a bucket of ice cream and tried to sell it to his mates in the bus. Of course they refused to buy as they knew he had stolen it and wanted it for free. In the end he had to relent and give it away before it melted.

I went to the home of one of the victims. I looked at this seventeen-year-old who looked thirteen and I couldn't imagine him drunk. He looked so small, like a little child to be sent to the shops, not like someone who could lift a beer can. He could not recall what happened. He was too drunk to know. Apparently he just lay there as he was being stabbed. His mother would not allow us to speak to him, saying they had been summoned to go to the police station.

"Except that I do not understand why our children who have been stabbed have to be questioned, when the police's job is to find the people responsible for all this fracas."

This woman's neighbor's son, aged fifteen, had been stabbed to death at the picnic. Another boy from the same street came home with a knife buried in his forehead, between the eyes. He was then taken to Baragwanath, where doctors performed a miraculous operation, but sadly they were unable to save his life. The woman said the police would not release the corpse to the parents, because they wanted to examine any possible "political" connections. She was very angry about this, asking since when do they keep corpses from the family.

We were listening to the woman when one of the neighbors' sons walked in. He had also been to the picnic. He said, "I heard my brother scream that this one was being injured and saw him rush to his assistance. The next thing a knife was plunged into my brother. The attacker ran off. I ran looking for transport to take the two to the hospital. Then there was chaos as the police came and chased people with tear gas. People were rushing to put their belongings together—provision baskets and music sets had to be packed in a hurry. There was tear gas smoke and bleeding people all around."

My friend and I moved from the victim's house to the local shops. We found a group engaged in conversation. I asked if they could explain what happened on Saturday. One of them wanted to know who I was. I mumbled that I was a reporter. He threw a copy of the *Citizen* at me and asked, "Did you write this?" I shook my head. I told him who I worked for. One of the boys took two steps and stood right in front of me, aggressively. "You are a comrade." he said. "Did you not raid so-and-so's house...?"

My palate went dry. He was referring to an occasion where I had been very embarrassed to find myself caught up, in the course of duty, in a raid by comrades. I had hoped against hope that nobody would remember me. But now it seemed the chickens were coming home to roost. I explained: "I am not a comrade. And I was at that house as a reporter. Just as I am here to listen to your side of the story." He seemed satisfied.

"What do you want to know? That we went out on a picnic and we were butchered like cows? I cannot tell you what happened but in the afternoon, we were all so high and there was our friend S'khumbuzo on the ground dead and others bleeding. It was bad," said a boy.

"We were enjoying ourselves, drinking beers and listening to music when two Portuguese guys arrived in a van selling liquor. By the evening many guys were drunk, and still they wanted more to drink. At that stage, most had run out of money. Some started playing rough with the Portuguese, wanting to take beers for free.

"A nasty scene was imminent so the police were called. They arrived and teargassed everyone. There was no transport to bring us back home as we had instructed our taxis to pick us up around six. So there we were, tear-gassed to go away—where to? anywhere. Some resisted being chased away and hit back at whatever was in their way. So here we are, without a brother and we don't even know who killed him."

I found out that the whole group were school-going kids. They were either doing standard nine or ten, and were between fifteen and twenty years old. They seemed to be into beer-drinking and, once drunk, they were uncontrollable. One of them, I was told, had tried to rape a girl not far from his home on returning from the picnic. In fact, the girl had been saved by his parents who came out on hearing the screams. It also transpired that one of the boys at the school they attend had decapitated a classmate, and that the other boys had spent an entire day combing the townships looking for the culprit.

An elderly witness claims the children were too drunk to know what was going on. He saw one being stabbed, and maintains it was to the good that they were so drunk. He lay there drunk while he was being stabbed. Had he been in his senses he would have pulled his own knife and there could have been another two deaths. As it was, the one ended up with many stab wounds in his buttocks.

135

The tragedy is the position of the parents. It is not as if parents do not know what happens at these picnics. They can do nothing about their children's behavior. How does the parent go against the tide? The kids have to protect themselves against many systems, using different weapons. At home, silence may be the best weapon to get nosy parents off one's back. At school, the choice is between killing time as best as one can and relying on the new slogan of "Pass One, Pass All," or getting on with the job and being resented as a "beterkoffie" or sellout. In the street it is either joining the gang (carrying knives, harassing girls and getting drunk) or be seen as a "barrie" (bum) and be humiliated for not being "with it."

On Saturday, S'khumbuzo should have been buried but the funeral did not take place because his mother died of a heart attack on Friday. His sister could not take it. She took poison and is being treated at Baragwanath Hospital.

October/November, 1987

Schooling: Quiet Collapse

WHEN WE FIRST heard the call for "Liberation now, Education later," we were told the students were going to stand united until liberation was achieved. What has happened is the opposite. The well-off children have left the township schools. The poor have stayed in the townships, where they have long forgotten education and now have forgotten liberation too. They roam the streets and only sometimes visit the classroom, where they meet their friends and play and chat. There is no secondary education any longer, in Soweto or in other main townships.

Every parent who can by any means afford it, has removed his/her children, sending them to private schools, homeland boarding schools or to live with relatives. There was a great deal of arm-twisting, begging and bribing. Among those to leave were students who incited others not to attend. That is one reason why there were no boycotts in 1987. Activists saw their way into private schools, where the spirit of militancy is subdued. At such schools they are overshadowed and outnumbered by their white colleagues. Added to that, the learning atmosphere is certainly different.

Aside from the "real" private schools, new schools mushroomed in the city. Students pay anything from R100 per month, and buy books as well as pay for transport into town. Now the township looks different. In the old days streets filled in the early mornings with children dressed in black-and-white uniforms. Today, there are minibuses ferrying children in the multi-colored uniforms of the white private schools. Another lot are the kids going by train and bus to the new schools in the city center, wearing clean casual gear. Later in the day come the remaining children from the township schools. They drift towards school at any time they like, wearing any outfit. Often they look more like thugs than schoolchildren.

During 1987 the school scene was ignored. At the beginning, everybody held their breath to see whether the kids would return to school. Some kids did not register immediately, but gradually it became obvious that they were back at school, and the politicians and newspapers began to lose interest. Sixteen June came and went without drama, and then people were finally convinced that the school problem was over.

Those who wanted to draw attention to the problems in the classrooms kept to themselves for fear of making waves just when life was returning to normal. Parents preferred to sweep the problems under the carpet. They were relieved that *sayinyova* had come to an end. The children were no longer rampaging and throwing stones. People did not want to disturb things by probing as to what was actually going on. They did not want to ask: why was there no homework any more? Why do the children go to school so late, and come back so early? They thought the less one knows, the better. If they did not look, the problem would disappear. But everybody knew, deep down, that things were wrong.

MR. H.H. DLAMLENZE, general secretary of the African Teachers Association of South Africa (ATASA) was regarded as a moderate and conservative until 1985, when he was detained for six months—because, he suspects, ATASA was planning a commemoration of the tenth anniversary of Soweto '76.

Although his tone has much changed, he is still basically a moderate. He continues living his life without lamenting the wasted time and humiliation of prison life. He does not speak with the usual ex-detainee rhetoric, and is not even proud of detention.

On the state of today's education he says, "I took a visiting American to a school and asked the principal if we could chat with students. The principal said it was all right with him but he first had to check with the SRC. My heart was sore. What has happened to authority? Who is leading whom?"

Mr. Dlamlenze maintains the teachers are powerless pawns in this game. The students want change and they want it now. The parents want the children out of the house and in someone else's care. The government wants to see them in the classroom to save face. Nobody is winning.

A lady teacher concurred, "Granted, we have no control over the students, but it is worse when you find some teachers currying favor with the children. The children get to expect that they can push teachers around. I have been approached on several occasions and threatened that I dare not let them fail my subject."

She cited a thirteen-year-old boy who had been absent from school for many weeks. Then he was brought back by his mother because he had raped a six-year-old. "His mother appealed to me to take him back to keep him out of harm's way. I had to take him because if I refused there could be a boycott—'an injury to one is an injury to all.'

"We are meant to be parents as well as teachers. Parents are too scared to preach about morals. They want us to do that, but we have no time set aside for it. The churches also shun that subject. They talk about the soul and preach against witchcraft and adultery, and hope the schools will explain to the growing child what is expected of him—without a syllabus for it!

"The new incoming teacher is a product of 1976. He fought the system as a student and did not get very far. He has an unfinished agenda which he passes on to the children. At times we cannot take important decisions that will affect the students, for fear that our colleagues might tell on us."

One teacher calls it "battle fatigue." The children are back at school physically and are recuperating from the four years of not learning. "Learning habits are broken down and it will be some years before we have a generation of children who are at school for the purpose of learning.

"Human beings are not taps that can be switched on and off, and the sooner the government learns that no amount of bullets will create a learning atmosphere the better. We have a generation that has been lost. What are we doing to save the next one?"

I called at a school that was one of the best in Soweto, at one point boasting of teachers with strings of degrees. It was also one of the high schools in the forefront of the 1976 uprisings. Today the school is a shadow of what it once was. The teachers openly describe themselves as "check collectors." They are destroyed.

"Soweto is Sodom and Gomorrah," says the headmaster. "This place must be razed to the ground and rebuilt afresh, and not with the present child. These children are poison."

If it was that bad, I said, why was he still teaching? The answer was simple. At over fifty, who would employ him? Because the department forbids teachers to give interviews, I cannot name him.

"Come and look at the children's scripts," he said. "They have written nothing because they have not been in the classroom. They have been coming to school when and if they want to. I have requested meetings with parents—these have not been attended. Parents are not interested in knowing whether their children are learning or not. As long as they seem to be away from home it is all right by them."

I looked at a pile of end-of-year exam scripts. What I saw was long blank spaces. A full sheet of paper could have three or four lines filled in. The rest had nothing but question numbers, with no answers next to them. "We also need to look at the social problems, such as the shortage of houses. People have been looting corrugated iron from my school to build shacks. When I confronted the ones I caught red-handed, they asked me, 'What does a child need most, a school or a home?' They said the school was not being used in any case, so why should they not strip the classrooms?"

He said, "In the past we felt hopeless with Bantu Education. Educationalists claimed that the longer a child stayed at school the more difficult it was to undo the harm done by Bantu Education. So year in and year out we churned out a frustrated product. But at least they knew their limitations and worked from that premise. Today, we have a zombie who comes to school, squanders his pocket money at break and goes home without having touched a book. The teacher can do nothing.

"Where does it put the black nation? We are going to be despised by everyone. Bantu Education was inferior, but at least a child received some education. In the past, whites sympathized with us because of the poor education we received. Now the opportunities are better, but the children have no goals, no values and no direction. They do not aspire to anything, they are just drifting along."

Another headmaster, a primary school principal, was one of the angriest people I have ever seen. A strong, athletic man, he has no fear, and he blames the collapse on "lily-livered" teachers. He said there was order in most primary schools. "We break our backs teaching and when our children leave our gates for high school, then we know it is good-bye to education. Teachers fear these kids. I have seen teachers being abused and humiliated by fifteen-year-olds and doing nothing about it."

I asked him about teachers who have been fatally assaulted by students. He said, "Fear will never solve our problems. A teacher must behave as one and not pander to the children's whims." A math teacher from a high school said: "We cannot continue fooling ourselves that we will wake up one day and find ourselves leading normal lives. Even teachers have taken their children away—you can't find a Soweto teacher whose child goes to a Soweto school. The government will continue to pretend all is well and keep on suppressing the lid. Education becomes available only to those who can afford private schools. We in the government schools continue collecting our checks to pay our bonds, but are not earning what we are paid."

I spoke to Mr. G.W. Merbold, regional director of the Department of Education and Training. His sole aim is to give the best education possible to the black child. He does not see education in this country as political and, "If you want to politicize it then you can go and talk to the politicians." In other words, he does not want to discuss the impact of political problems on education. He points out that at least in 1987, 83 percent of registered children did actually sit for the exams.

"I am not very optimistic about the results because the studying patterns of pupils had broken down and we could not water down the examinations to suit the children. We have no intention of bringing down the standards lest we be accused of offering an education that is inferior."

He said black children were receiving free education, of the same quality as white people. There were no school fees paid by parents, and pupils were being given free stationery and books. All a black child had to do was present him- or herself to the school and study. The only payment required of parents was the school fund, which was determined by the school and which was voluntary anyway.

"And yet some parents prefer to pay exorbitant amounts at the schools in town."

I asked why would parents pay exorbitant amounts if they could get good education free. He said, "You tell me, I don't understand the people's mentality. They run away from schools in black areas, claiming they are getting away from DET, but at the end of the year they sit for our exams."

I said that if black and white education was equal, what was the point of having different departments? He said that was a question, not for him, but for the politicians. He said parity had been reached in pay, subsidies and pension schemes.

Mr. Merbold genuinely felt he was doing the right thing for the people, but whether the people realized that, was another matter. It is not the changing of the name of Bantu Education to DET that people wanted. The people were calling for one education for all South African children, and parity in spending. We have seen the many schools that have been built and the free stationery, but these have not meant better learning.

The department wants to normalize education without dealing with the basic political problems. To me, that is a waste of time. It is not a matter of whether 83 percent or any other percentage of children are sitting in classrooms, it is a matter of whether they are learning how to hold their own in society.

How Mr. Merbold can claim to be doing the best for the black child, while he refuses to see the core of the problem, is beyond me. All we are going to have is a cycle of lulls and then storms. The difference is not between progress and collapse. It is between quiet collapse and violent collapse.

CAME JANUARY 1988 and matric results were announced. There was more skepticism than jubilation. Although there has been a marginal increase in the pass rate—from 53 percent to 56 percent—as well as an increase in the number of university entrances, black parents are not excited. They smell a rat. People feel that somehow the results are being cooked. For one thing, the director of education, Mr. M.G. Merbold, predicted an improvement on the result. Indeed, the result came out better. This was in spite of the lack of learning and the noncommitment of children towards education.

Parents are asking who the department is fooling, because the situation in Soweto has been such that everybody knew what was going on, and yet the result came out as though there has been an effort towards learning. Of course, the children had gone back to school, but whether they were learning anything is another matter. One teacher spoke of "letting the stream flow," which she claimed was a directive from the department that they should allow kids to proceed to the next class so as not to create bottlenecks at high school.

And from the looks of things the situation is going to remain unredressed because already black leaders who would be in a position to tackle the department do not have their children in Soweto schools. They do not feel comfortable speaking on behalf of the ordinary parent whose child is schooling in the township. They have been criticized for wanting to represent other people's children while theirs were not at such schools. So who is going to confront the department?

Already parents are running to and fro trying to find schools outside Soweto. There has been an even larger group of students leaving black schools for the ones in town. Even those in town have experienced a shift from one school to the other. This is in spite of the good results that are alleged to have come out. Where there should have been an exodus of children going back to the ghetto schools, we see them drifting even further away. And the truth of the matter is, children who want to learn have no confidence in black schools.

THE REMAINDER OF THIS CHAPTER CONSISTS OF THREE ANECDOTES, WHICH WE REPRODUCE SEPARATE FROM THE BODY OF THE TEXT.

I SPOKE TO a girl who tried to write matric in 1985. She was turned back by comrades. Her back bears testimony, showing marks from the *shambokking* she got when she crossed the boycott line.

Once more in 1986 she enrolled to write, but they were again told there would be no writing of examinations. This time she did not bother to get to the center. Came 1987, she registered with both the Adult Center and the day school.

"A teacher with a first period will find that he has three or five students to teach. Suppose he decides to teach, then he has to teach the same thing the next day to those children who were not there the previous day. The following day he may be faced with a different lot. So what do the teachers do? They stay out of class, especially those with early periods. And I don't blame them," she said.

Although her back has black marks from the beatings, she is not bitter. "At first I was very angry. My mother was away at work and I wanted to commit suicide. I was in terrible pain. I couldn't find tablets or medicine to drink to kill myself. I cried myself to sleep. When my mother came back my entire back was swollen. She broke down and together we wept. She was worse than me because she kept on calling my father's name asking why did he have to die and leave her with such problems. We felt so helpless. I could not even call any of my male cousins for help because those were the days when students who had braved the comrades and sat for exams were viewed as sellouts. In the meantime, children in other parts of the country were writing as though nothing was happening.

AT ORLANDO HIGH I met a girl of about twenty, who I found out was writing matric. She started school in 1974. Since then she has experienced seven years of learning ('74-'75, '79-'83), five years of disruption ('76-'77, '84-'86) and two years of limbo ('78 and '87). As a primary school child in '76 and '77, her school was closed several times either because high school students came to chase children away, or because there was shooting or tear gas in the vicinity and the principal sent them home.

"In 1984 the comrades told us not to come to school. They would tear our books and gym dresses. Soon soldiers came into the school grounds and not long after that the school was shut down.

"My parents applied to boarding schools, but they would not

take me from Johannesburg as I would be a bad influence. I went to a private school.

"When schools were reopened I went back. Some of us were against what the comrades were doing. When we used to confront them about 'liberation now and education later' they would tell us to go to the classroom at our own risk, and *that* we dared not do.

"Students today do as they please. A class can be busy at work in one classroom only to find the next room behaving as if it was a picnic. Loud music is played and boys and girls frolic about. If you don't like that scene, you are advised to get out of the classroom. Most teachers don't bother to come after lunch because there are no children to teach.

"This causes problems for us girls who want to study. It is for this reason that we have formed study groups and conduct house visits. It is not safe for girls to study on their own at school. Some have been raped in the classrooms.

"Everything is left up to the student. Some of the students who were in the front of *nyovment* are studying again. But there are those who do not want to learn. I have enrolled with the night school in case the call comes again for us to leave the class-rooms."

I VISITED THULARE High School in White City Jabavu. This is one of the double-story buildings which was built after 1976. In the old days, schools were long, single-story "L" shapes, white at the top and maroon below. The new pattern makes schools look different, like barracks.

Thulare stands impressively next to the ecumenical centers of the Lutheran and Methodist churches, which give it, from the out-side, an appearance of calm and dignity.

Inside, the school is filthy and run down. Some classrooms are without doors. Broken desks lie all over the place. An attempt is made to sweep the floors, but the whole place is grey from lack of polish. The walls compete for inscriptions of rival polit-ical groups. The ceiling is marked by ball prints creating a mud-dy tapestry of what once was a white ceiling. The toilets are no longer used because they are not cleaned. Before the uprisings, students took turns in cleaning toilets. Today there is no child who is prepared to clean toilets.

I went to Orlando High School. For years this school was the pride of Soweto. It has been fondly referred to as "the Rock." Many great people were educated there and some of the best teachers taught there—Prof. Ezekiel Mphahlele, Mr. Godfrey Pitje and Mr. Ike Moephuli, to mention but a few.

For many years the great Mr. T.W. Khambule was principal. Although Orlando High is in the heart of crime country, it always stood above crime. Order was its language.

Today many classrooms and toilets (always a separate building) are without roofs as the corrugated iron has been stolen. In some classes, tiles on the floor have been removed and the ceiling in the staff room has been taken.

January, 1988

The Empire Strikes Back

SOME SAY THE chickens are coming home to roost. Some say people have had a two-year Christmas—paying no rent for all that time, they are supposed to be rich by now. Some say they are stupid and wonder how long they hoped to live rent-free. The residents say "we have been robbed."

One thing is for sure. The great rent boycott is collapsing. People used to expect that there would be a big dramatic clampdown. They said that the government would never succeed, because it would face united resistance from a million people. But the government has chosen "softly, softly catchee monkey."

All the time, the people have waited for the leaders and the government to come to some agreement. But now the leaders are silenced or silent. The drama has gone, and it has become a matter of the Soweto Council police, protected by the army, picking on selected spots and leaving people rushing to pay the rent.

This month they raided houses in Chiawello 3, demanding rent receipts. Those who did not have current receipts had their furniture thrown into the army trucks and their homes locked up. People were running backwards and forwards looking for leaders, looking for money, pointing fingers at those who were not raided. Streets were piled with televisions, sofas, fridges, food. Women wailed hopelessly. Children watched as their beds were flung into trucks. The constables loaded, under the watch of the soldiers who casually chomped on fruit or sipped drinks from the fridge. The sound of splintering and cracking rang out. Drawers fell out of cupboards, and clothes and cutlery fell out of drawers.

For many months Chiawello residents have been unhappy with the boycott. They have wanted to pay rent, and get rid of the insecurity. But they couldn't just go and pay, they needed to have the problem resolved. Chiawello 3 has been cursed with rent confusion since the township was built in 1982. Residents were told they would pay R145.20 provisional rent for six months. Then the amount would be reviewed.

After six months, nothing was done about reducing the rent. The people's grievance was that they were paying the highest rent of any township—for houses that were not worth it. The houses are three bedrooms, kitchen, living room, toilet and bathroom. They are one brick structure, no flooring and no ceiling. There is no geyser. Tenants must plaster the inside walls to cover the unsightly mazista bricks. They have to close the gaps on the asbestos roofing, and put up their own ceiling. There is no guarantee that occupants will be reimbursed for expenses incurred to make the houses habitable. And yet the law states that the landlord must make sure that a house is habitable before tenants can move in.

People did pay the provisional rent for four years. During that time they made the houses habitable. There was much discontent, particularly since those who tried to buy their homes were told they were overvalued. The Soweto Council wanted R11,000 to R13,000, but building societies would not give loans, saying the houses' value was R6,000. Representation was made to the Soweto Council to no avail. The residents gave the council an ultimatum to review the rent or they would stop paying. They told the councillors that they were prepared to compromise by letting them treat the money they had been robbed of as deposits towards buying the homes. But all that fell on deaf ears and in March 1986, Chiawello 3 residents stopped paying rent.

Two months later the rest of Soweto did the same thing, although for different reasons. It was a crucial time. Street committees were being formed, students were boycotting classes, and necklacing was common. Council police as well as councillors were being attacked. In Chiawello 3 for instance, a constable who was notorious for his sadistic raiding methods had his house gutted by fire. The fear of God came to constables and the councillors as well. House raids came to a stop. Councillors fled from Soweto and took refuge in town. The Council police (blackjacks) were suddenly seen moving about the township with rifles. This was a strange phenomenon, for not even the much feared SAP (South African Police) carry rifles. Only soldiers display rifles.

The months that followed were confusing. Rumors spread like fire—payments would be credited towards home-ownership; rent would be reduced; evictions were coming; other townships were paying rents secretly. In some areas refuse was not collected, and water and electricity came on and off. Some people said we could rest easy, because the government would do nothing to us until they had dealt with the Vaal boycott, which was three years older.

The Chiawello 3 issue was not part of the greater Soweto boycott. Some elements were for dialogue with the Soweto Council, but the day was won by those who refused to recognize the councillors, saying they were placed by the government and not elected by the people. Another school would not hear of paying rent until Mandela and other political prisoners were released. A large part of their argument was that black people had no other means of communicating.

To some people this was downright stupid. They did not understand what rent had to do with politics. The proponents of the boycott said: "Was the creation of Soweto not politics? Where else could you find a landlord renting a house that is a health hazard and not being hurled to court? Where in the world do you find that the government is the landlord? Where except in South Africa would you find these conditions pertaining only to one section of its community? Where else would one find security forces deployed to deal with rent defaulters?"

On 27 August 1986, White City residents clashed with municipal police and the army. Twenty-seven people died. Again, stories circulated like wildfire. Many said that armed ANC cadres had ambushed the police. Some said that local youths had been warned that evictions were to take place, and had prepared caches of stones to fight. A few months later, the scene was almost repeated in Phomolong. Someone blew the "help" whistle and out came innocent tenants, thinking it was a genuine cry. Four died that night.

Came 1987, there was still uncertainty. People started to receive electricity and water bills only, with no rent statements. Evictions increased. There would be new rumors every few weeks, about different townships—now Emndeni, now Naledi, now Zola. At that point, street committees were no longer functioning, because leaders had been detained. There was no longer any coordination between the people and the comrades. People ceased to think in terms of street committees, and one by one, they started paying. No one would publicly admit to paying rent, but it was obvious that many were. People gave all sorts of excuses for being seen at the offices.

Some people paid so as to get taxi licenses. "When I went for my license they wanted my current latest rent receipt. I had to pay." Others paid when they went for permits to build onto their homes. Acquiring the ninety-nine-year lease also required up-to-date payment.

Chiawello residents received letters informing them that the rent issue was under review and tenants would be hearing from the council soon. This gave residents hope. But nothing more happened. People did not know how much they owed. Main roads acquired billboards which to this day still read: "Water is a bargain, but even bargains must be paid for." The same was said of electricity, housing and transport. The inference was that residents do not want to pay. But this is wrong. What we want is to solve the problem so that we can pay. The houses appearing on the advert are, strangely enough, not the rented four-room structures, but the new development houses found in exclusive parts.

People became angry about the "bargain" advertisements, because water and electricity bills are astronomical. They are much higher than white homes, and the story is that we pay more per unit because the white areas have already paid off their infrastructure.

Besides, since the riots started in 1985 there has been no meter reader. How do they arrive at their figures? An average bill reads from R150 to R200. As for saying a rickety and dirty Putco bus is a bargain, that is beyond imagination. In Chiawello a taxi to town costs ten cents less than a bus.

We welcomed 1988 with hope. People prayed that the rent issue would be resolved. Then the Soweto Council started cracking the whip. They evicted people in certain areas of Chiawello 1 and 2, most of whom were pensioners. One was left out in the cold for the night and has since died from exposure.

Then one bright summer morning in Chiawello 3 residents were rudely awakened. There was a contingent. They wanted rent. The soldiers stood pointing rifles while officials demanded the current receipts. People mumbled a promise and were told that the soldiers would be back the following Thursday and woe betide defaulters.

Some residents rushed to pay or make a pledge to pay. Came the fateful Thursday and the officials kept their promise. Those who had not paid had their furniture taken to the superintendent's office. By evening there was chaos. The township was divided. Some had paid, some wanted to pay but had no money, some demanded solidarity in the name of the original Chiawello issue. Others demanded solidarity in the name of the bigger political issue.

Meetings were called. One went off well in the sense that it did take place although nothing came out of it. The next was disrupted by the arrival of the police who demanded a letter from the commissioner of police giving permission to hold the meeting.

Ultimately, a group of women marched to the Soweto Council chambers where they confronted the housing officer, Miss Estelle Bester. She uncompromisingly told them that unless the residents paid rent, including backlog, they would be put out on the street.

There is confusion in most townships of Soweto. But none is as bad as in Chiawello 3. They have not achieved anything from the boycott. Instead they have a huge backlog to pay. The various committees that were set up have folded as people voted no confidence in them. Every evening spells nightmare for some. Others have lost important and expensive pieces of furniture. Some have not recovered some of the items taken away, even after paying.

The leaders are behind bars or saying nothing. A few cases are with lawyers. The rest of the people wait for their fate to be decided, by the superintendents, town clerk Nico Malan, housing officer Ms. Bester, Mayor Botile and the councillors. They are the Pontius Pilates in this matter.

February, 1988

Appointment
with the Hangman

*WRITTEN 17 MARCH 1988, THE DAY BEFORE THE SCHEDULED EXE-
CUTION OF THE "SHARPEVILLE SIX."*

THEY SAY HOPE springs eternal in the human breast and that where
there is life, there is hope. For relatives of condemned people,
these are not jokes.

From the moment the judge pronounces the death sentence, those
involved carry the fear and anxiety like an invisible cross. They
will spend the rest of their lives asking questions: "Was he really
hanged?" or "Is it true that they are kept somewhere in the bowels
of the earth minting money?" or "Why are we never shown the
bodies?" (There are strong rumors in black circles that people are
not hanged but incarcerated in some building in Pretoria, manu-
facturing money. This myth is strengthened by claims that no one
has ever come out of the black community who has actually professed to be working or having worked in a minting factory.)

After the initial shock of the sentence, when the mother or wife
has recovered, these women will temporarily wipe their tears away,
pick up their skirts and move Heaven and earth to save their dear
ones from the gallows. Once more, lawyers are consulted, special
prayers held at times, *inyangas* are consulted. No stone is left un-
turned.

The next shock comes when the date of the hanging is announced. The judge's words drum through your head. I have known

a third shock. A lawyer who has been working hard on an appeal said, "I think he is going to be hanged. They have called me asking for his measurements." I was thunderstruck. Later, I found out that apparently they feel it would be too crude to measure him in jail.

The worst of all days is the day before the hanging. Death is a mystery. Although we live in the shadow of death, somehow we never get used to it. One may have a very sick relative and be reconciled to the fact that he may die at any minute. But when the time actually comes, the very people who had accepted the inevitable, reject the reality.

Accepting hanging is difficult. The fact that one may die from choking on food or from a motor car accident is one thing. Knowing that someone, somewhere is a special person who lives among people—a father, perhaps a lover, maybe a warm-natured person, a respectable citizen who stops for old ladies to pass, who never says anything untoward to anyone—and knowing that that person is the one who turns the switch that severs life from a person is even harder to be reconciled with.

Since the issue lies in the hands of someone with power, somehow the victim and all those involved nurse the hope until the last minute that there might just be a change of heart from the people who wield power. I saw an old woman of seventy, a Christian all her life, lose faith and belief in the Almighty because of a son who was executed. She came out of the chapel after being shown coffins, one of which held her son's remains. Fancy for the preacher to lie to us and say our children have been called by God, when they have killed them in front of us. Only a white God does that.

The eve before the hanging is the most cruel day for those visiting Pretoria Maximum Prison. That day, all concerned try by any means to visit their dear ones. People come from all over the country. Some come from as far away as Cape Town or Zululand and may be spending the night at the prison. Waiting-cum-sleeping rooms await those without accommodation at neighboring townships. There are usually one or two whites to hang and a host of blacks. The place is always swarming with black, Indian and Coloured people. It is not possible to see condemned white people because, true to South African tradition, their cells are at some distance. One wonders if they use different colored people as hangmen.

THE LARGE DOUBLE doors open with the clang of metal. Behind the screen are huge men in blue uniforms. Someone once remarked that nowhere can you find Boers as big as the ones at Pretoria Maximum. Tall, hefty, with blue eyes, they give visitors long, cold stares as they ask for the name of the prisoner, and then let them through. Security is so tight, they never bother to ask for the visitors' particulars. There is nothing a visitor could do to help anybody escape once he is in there. You walk along the peaceful, long passage in one of the cleanest prisons in South Africa, maybe in the whole of the continent. There are broad, tarred lanes where sometimes one can see a contingent of black men with shining heads, in prisoner's clothes, going through their exercises.

Out there, your eyes are also enchanted by well-manicured, sprawling lawns and flowers. No one watches over you, but the feeling of being watched is with you all the time. As you walk in that corridor of death, you make a silent prayer that none of your remaining dear ones ever give you cause to come here. You want to turn back and lecture your son and all your nephews. You will do that later. For now, you have to be strong and face the one to be hanged. There is nobody to escort visitors. Somehow, you follow the crowd. After all, there is only one reason you are all here. There is no rush here.

Some talk in subdued tones. Others drift along like zombies up to the visitors' reception area. The most humane black policemen are to be found here. They are the first to greet visitors, sometimes they even ask after your health. They don't seem to have grown used to anguish. They are important people because tradition has it that on the eve of hanging, the one to hang the next day offers sweets to those remaining. The policemen are the ones who buy the sweets with the money left as gifts to the prisoners.

Every step one takes on that day is a step of hope. Hope that something drastic may happen. But, as one enters the room and takes a place at one of the windows, one is enveloped by the great fear that it is your brother's, sister's, husband's or friend's last day on earth. You wrestle with hope against hope that maybe it is not. You ask yourself the question: "What do I say to him?" You stand by the window next to the microphone while he is being called. Next to you, a conversation might be in progress between a relative and a condemned person. You are able to hear all they are saying. Soon the prisoner you have come to see will emerge from the passage in front of where you are standing. He will be a picture of health. Remember, they are fed well and the condemned are not worked. He will be clean-shaven, in immaculate khaki shirt and shorts. He may be carrying a Bible.

Your eyes will meet and you will look down, perhaps to stop a tear or not to let him see that you are about to cry. Maybe at that stage he will start a familiar hymn and fellow prisoners will join in and the whole place will become a church. Someone preaches. It's amazing how much of a blanket worshipping becomes. With everyone desperately trying not to crack, they cling to the flimsy, invisible anchor of Christianity. There will be those who are overcome by emotion, and let the tears stream down their cheeks. Some will faint and be carried outside. There is no screaming.

Those to hang may be musing or speaking softly to relatives, giving last-minute instructions on what is to be done after they have been executed. If he is a father, the prisoner will ask after the children who are underage, who are not allowed to visit prisons. And perhaps his wife may have brought pictures of the children and show them to him through the glass barrier. He will then tell his wife to look after the children, and ask her to make sure they go to church and to school. One by one, relatives and friends will go to the window and have something to say to him. At this stage, the prisoners are on another plane. They have made peace with their Creator and are telling visitors how they are looking forward to meeting Him. They console their dear ones and tell them to be brave and wait for the day when they'll meet. They all have smiling faces, perhaps dancing and singing to the hymns.

These may have been rapists or guerrillas or thugs who have murdered. But, before the crowd then, they are loved ones who will be seen for the last time that morning or afternoon. Beneath the veneer of Christianity, of bravery, of anxiety to meet one's God, there is still hope. Hope that the lawyers may pull out a card. Hope that some sudden new evidence may prove one's innocence. Hope that somewhere, people in power may just have a rethink.

BENEATH THAT VENEER, one asks all sorts of questions. Just as one is asking questions today as the "Sharpeville Six" wait for tomorrow's appointment with the hangman. How can a judge sentence people to death based on circumstantial evidence? How can one be executed for being part of a crowd? How many more such deaths will there be before this country wakes up to realizing that capital punishment will not bring peace? That jails will not stop people from demanding their rights as citizens?

The fact that the six will meet the hangman simply because someone said they were there makes me shudder. I have lived with all sorts of violence. I was once attacked by a group of ten or twelve men and watched helplessly as they looted food, clothing and money from my house. I was lucky not to have been raped or maimed. My children had to live through that ordeal. I have seen a person stabbed and die before my helpless eyes. I have seen a political mob at work, and I have seen people being dragged into actions they would not like to have done. I have seen twelve-year-olds threaten old and helpless people. During the first months of the rent boycott, I listened to an old woman tell how youngsters harassed her for an entire evening for having paid her rent. They broke every glass and all the furniture in her house, playing trampoline on her sofa and bed.

I once watched fifteen-year-olds beat up a girl of twelve whose crime had been going to school when a boycott was declared. They made a bonfire of her books and her uniform. She was released to go home in her panties. I know of teenagers who were collected from homes for meetings to discuss the struggle. What do you do when you are told to necklace an informer, and refusing implies that you are condoning sellouts, and that, therefore, your own home will be gutted? How many strong men have surrendered the keys to their vehicles at the threats of children? How many youngsters languish in prison for crimes they did not commit—

victims of informers who had run out of stories, victims of petty jealousies and witch-hunting? It could have been my daughter or son seen with the mob, and someone decided to tell the cops. I shudder.

At the height of the "comrade mania," my sister was stopped by youths for driving a "target," meaning a car belonging to a white company. It was forcefully taken away from her and she had to find her way home alone. Later, she was subpoenaed. At court, she was surprised to be shown a strange boy as the one who had taken the car. She told the prosecutor she had never seen the accused before. No amount of persuasion (friendly or otherwise) from the prosecutor could make her say different. The boy was acquitted. It turned out later that the boy had nothing to do with the youths who had terrorized my sister. In fact, they had decided to nail him with the crime because he had resisted joining them.

In 1976, when the security police were detaining students, they visited the home of an activist in the street where I used to live. When they got to the boy's home, his mother denied she had a son with that name. She said that the Vusi they were looking for lived at house number such-and-such, down the road. When the police got to that house, no questions were asked. The poor boy was bungled into the van and spent over eighteen months in prison. He is now twenty-seven years old, suffers from high blood pressure, is without matric, and without a job. A bitter man.

We know the story of the "Soweto Eleven," who paid for the crimes that took place during 1976. We know that there was no evidence against them, except for the fact that they were the student leaders. There was not a single witness who saw any of the eleven lift a stone to cause anyone any harm. Nor was there a witness who saw any one of the eleven set a building alight. They were guilty of being leaders and of addressing meetings which, the court alleged, incited the students to go on a rampage. They spent two years awaiting trial.

Some were acquitted while others were given a jail sentence. That, unfortunately, is justice according to the whites in South Africa. For as long as blacks are not part of the governing body, and as long as the law is designed by whites without blacks, and the judiciary displays insensitivity as has been happening lately, and as long as white soldiers can, because of Botha's protection, get away with crimes such as the killing of innocent civilians in Namibia, while black rioters are sent to the gallows on flimsy or nonexistent evidence, then hope and security for this country will remain a pipe dream.

Instead, we are sure to see more blacks going to Pretoria Maximum Prison, either as visitors or to keep their appointments with the hangman.

EDITOR'S NOTE: On 23 November 1988, State President P.W. Botha commuted death sentences of the "Sharpeville Six" to prison terms ranging from eighteen to twenty-five years. The action came only hours after the Appeals Court unanimously rejected an appeal to reopen the trial of the six defendants.

The "Sharpeville Six"—Mojalefa Reginald Sefatsa, Francis Mokgesi, Reid Mokoena, Oupa Moses Diniso, Duma Joshua Khumalo and Theresa Ramashamole—were convincted of murder in connection with the September 1984 mob killing of a black town councillor, Kuzwayo Dlamini, in Sharpeville, a township south of Johannesburg.

Although there was actually no evidence presented linking any of the six to the councillor's murder, the five men and one woman were sentenced to death under the doctrine of "common purpose," which held them responsible because of their alleged participation in the riot (which began after another rent increase was announced).

According to the group's lawyer, a further appeal for clemency is now in process.

March, 1988

159

Tato's Funeral:
Reflections
from the Graveside

I HAVE BEEN to many funerals. I have been to those where on returning from the graveyard, I have thrown myself on my bed, drained. I have been to some where I was merely performing a duty, and to others simply to satisfy curiosity, as though to say: "Is he really dead," or "What will the funeral be like?"

I have also been lured into attending funerals. What do you do when you visit a sister only to find she is on her way to the funeral of a person you hardly know? She persuades you to go along by sermonizing, "One day you will be dead and people won't come to your funeral." Who cares? I will be too dead to care, but I go with her anyway.

There are other ways of being hijacked to funerals. During the 1976 uprisings, students would force motorists to drive them to the cemeteries to bury their comrades. Looking back, that was nothing compared to what happened ten years later. Then you were not made to go to the funeral, but you did not expect to see your car again. You would be left at the roadside watching your car disappear into the distance with a driver working out the difference between break and clutch and twenty shouting passengers.

I HAVE JUST buried Tato. And yet I don't feel like I have just come from a funeral. Not that there was no solemn hymn singing and the usual "ashes to ashes" bit. No, everything was there. Hearse, cortege, wreaths, artificial green grass where the chief mourners are to sit by the graveside, Soweto's "who's who," and to crown it all, three dignified bishops of the True Church of Christ in Zion of South Africa in Soweto. They led the procession in their flowing maroon and black silk gowns. They took turns preaching. This was done very demonstratively, the voices changing gears as the spirit moved them, climaxed by interjections of a long sonorous A-M-E-N.

And yet I still do not feel that I have been to a funeral. This is in spite of the confusion and the rowdy business. On one side, the ethereal, angelic Catholics or Anglicans who are hushly doing their thing. On another side, the Salvation Army's Christian Soldiers' brass band deafens us all. On a third side is an indigenous traditional congregation whose big women shriek heaven high adding new notes to the total distortion of John Wesley's creation, while their baritone backup of heavily bearded guys lends dignity to the occasion. Shovels at work here, the last post being played there. A siren pierces through the commotion, announcing the arrival of yet another funeral. People hurry to their cars. Those who manage to make it to the gates first leave gales of red dust behind as testimony to a job done and the need to get away. Bus drivers rev their engines impatiently while passengers scramble for seats. Township funerals.

So Tato is dead. It is not that I do not believe it. However, I cannot come to grips with it. I can imagine him laughing at a shebeen as we talk of his funeral. He would certainly be the first to laugh at his lifeless body in the coffin. Tato, *kawufane ucinge*—just imagine, Tato dead.

At the graveside, when it was time for the body to descend to its final resting place—until the sound of the trumpet shall ring for all—the coffin would not go down. The poor undertaker's face was marked with beads of sweat. He did not know what to do. He kept fidgeting with the button that controls the lever to pull the coffin. Soon he had to abandon the fancy modern gadget and resort to the good-old-fashioned ropes that he had to fetch from the car, leaving the coffin hanging suspended half in midair. We had all thought it was a technical problem until someone remarked, "Trust Tato to refuse to go down without a fuss." People chuckled. But then another one was quick to say, "No, you are missing the point kid, you forget that Tato had no time for old spinsters. He wouldn't go down on a hymn initiated by old Miss Pooe."

Now that made sense. During the tension, as the coffin refused to go down and the African sun competed with the demands of dignity, the singing had stopped. A well-known lady with a remarkable voice (nicknamed "Lena Horne") saved the day. She started singing the popular funeral hymn "*Jerusalema e motsha*" ("The New Jerusalem"). By the time the undertaker came back with the ropes there was a roaring congregation. In no time, Tato was out of sight, down there. He probably waved us goodbye as he descended to his last place of abode, as they say.

Tato also loathed teetotallers. Once at a friend's funeral vigil, a drunk took the floor. He was supposed to give tribute to the deceased. Instead, he began a long sob story about himself saying things such as, "I have really lost a friend. I wonder with whom shall I share my nip of brandy now that Masondo is dead." He went on and on, much to the embarrassment of the audience and annoyance of the master of ceremonies who stopped him short: "Thank you brother, that will be enough, please sit down. This is no place for drunks."

Tato saw red. He stood up and demanded, "What right have you to belittle my friend when he is expressing his feelings about someone he knew and loved. You, who can hardly lift an empty beer glass. What do you know about the deceased? And as for you," he turned pointing to the man who had sat down, "you shall never have another opportunity to give praise to our friend. Come and say your piece."

The man stood up and continued with his speech as though nothing had happened. He went on to say, "I envy his wife Mampinga who will soon get a man to share the huge double bed and the long cold nights with," and sat down sobbing profusely. He was escorted out of the tent and given a stiff tot of brandy.

I MET TATO many years ago at a wedding. There was this immaculate man at my table dressed in old-style formality. His well-trimmed grey hair set like a halo on a face that bore lines of wisdom. We had just finished eating the usual sumptuous wedding luncheon when Tato said to the man next to him: "My friend,

I am not in the habit of eating and moving off without thank-
ing my host." Standing up and fixing his out-dated tuxedo and
clearing his moustache of crumbs, he moved to the bridal table.

*"Manene Namanenekazi, ndiyabulela kwaba bantwana ude bafike
kulomgangatho onina noyise abangakhange bafunyelele kuwo."* He
shook hands with the couple and walked away leaving the guests
roaring with laughter.

Apparently both the groom and the bride were children born
out of wedlock. Both pairs of parents had never gotten round to
getting married. So Tato had congratulated the couple for doing
better than their parents.

After he had left, I was among the many who wanted to know
who the witty old man was and the answer we got was that he
was Tata Mthimkulu, generally known as Tato.

I was later to meet him at all sorts of places. I would collide
with him at funerals, political rallies, soccer matches, shebeens,
almost everywhere, and always he was the jolly old man with
a bag full of funny stories.

He professed to know everybody. He claimed to have been in
the ANC when it was formed, the PAC when it broke off from
the ANC and BCM when it was started. Can you believe that?
Who wouldn't believe Tato once he started talking. In most cases
it wasn't so much believing what he said but being mesmerized
with the manner in which he spoke.

He would make fun of everybody, including himself. One of
the best shows he put up was when imitating Potlako Leballo of
PAC smoking a tobaccoless pipe at the old Synagogue in Pretoria
during the Great Treason Trial. Who were we to argue with him
when we hardly knew the people? He was our mirror to our heroes.

In his style he would brag and tell us how he'd brushed shoulders
with so-and-so, people we only read about in history books. Of
course he was on first name terms with them all.

Another masterpiece was his narration of his wedding night.
"And there was Mamtolo huddled up in the corner with her big
eyes as though about to fall off." He would emit a hearty laugh.
"Seeing her coiled up like an embryo I lost my temper and said,
"Hlala kahle man, andina kutya" ("Sit properly man, I am not
about to eat you up"). If anybody asked him why he was angry

with a frightened young girl from the homelands thrust into an arranged marriage with a man twice her senior, he said, "That night in particular I was in no mood for a virgin." Although Tato had come to Johannesburg at a very tender age and had practically grown up in the city, when it came to choosing a wife, his parents had organized a bride for him. So he was torn between maintaining tradition and forfeiting his township lovers. Nor was it any better for the girl. She was to spend the rest of her life with this man who was a stranger to her as well as acclimate herself to township life.

Tato got along with everybody. He seemed to have an understanding for all people. "My boy, never play around with a tsotsi. Tsotsis have no scruples," was one of his bits of advice. He would then tell his favourite tsotsi/mfundisi joke. The story was of a punter pastor, who borrowed money from a tsotsi on a hot tip. But something slipped up and his horse did not come in. The pastor could not meet his obligation towards the tsotsi.

"On the Sunday he should have paid the tsotsi," narrated Tato, "Mfundisi preached on Jesus' entry to Jerusalem, how he commanded his disciples to get him a donkey. Meanwhile from the pulpit he could see through the window. The tsotsi was standing outside with a knife, gesticulating to him demanding his money.

"With his hands in the air, the pastor said, 'Jesus did not have the means of transport. Bazalwane, when someone says he does not have, he means just that. And people must understand. I mean, I don't have. Understand?'

"Outside the tsotsi could hear every word said inside. He pointed the knife in the direction of the pastor who got the message and said, '*Nhlanganiso enhle* (good congregation) I shall now have the collection and conclude, as I have somewhere to go lest you attend my funeral.' Somehow the tsotsi got his money back."

Tato never went to church. His reason: "I do not want to go to heaven when I die, fancy meeting Ou Strydom, Smuts, Malan, Verwoerd and who's the ancestor of the Boers? Ja, the great pirate Ou Jan van Riebeeck and his fancy hairdo.

"What if I should find there is separate development out there? No. I want to go down there and meet my ancestors. The guy I really am looking forward to meeting to iron out a few things with is Shaka. Boy, if only he'd lived longer, we'd be talking of a different South Africa. I'd be some roving Foreign Affairs minister confusing everybody wherever I go.

"I'd also like to meet the great Moshoeshoe and congratulate him on his stone-throwing techniques. Heaven knows where Leabua Jonathan would be if Moshoeshoe had not gone up Thaba Bosiu and kept rolling them down. Jonathan would still be down there in the pits of the earth singing *Abelungu, ngo damn, basibiza ngo Jim.* Today he sits pretty well.

"I'd meet the mothers of Africa. I will have quite a time getting to know them.

"And if you ask me what shall I tell them on where I come from, I do not have the answer. Shall I tell them that we are busy wasting time splitting hairs over nothing, killing each other for no reason?" Each time he spoke like that, clouds would gather in his eyes and even those who tend to laugh over nothing knew that Tato had entered another plane.

"What has happened to us? Why are we killing each other so much? Look at the witch hunting and the backbiting that is happening all around us. Why can't we sit down and talk of the problems instead of destroying each other? No," he would say, shaking his head as though talking to himself (and maybe he was). "The fault is not with us. We are but pawns in the game. Where in the world have you seen a nation that has been denied its leaders like we have? All the nations in the world have people they look up to but us. Even animals have the lion to look up to. What do we have?

"What happens to children in a home without parents? Why are we expected to be different? Everyone is faced with his or her day-to-day struggle and the larger struggle is meant to take care of itself. Is there any wonder we are tearing each other up the way we do?"

On such occasions, Tato would leave unceremoniously and those who knew him grew to appreciate not to bother him.

Tato was very crude in dishing out what he regarded as advice. His nephew told him he had been offered a better job but could not bring himself to resign and leave his employer in the lurch. Tato hit the roof.

"From today, you must stop telling people that you are my relation," he screamed. "I don't even want to know you. Get out of my sight. You disgust me.

"Fancy feeling sorry for leaving your baas. When will black people ever be liberated, *nnxh*," emitting air from the back part of his half empty gums. "Do they ever feel sorry for you when they fire you?

"I used to know real liberated guys. For instance there was this guy who went to a Portuguese shop to buy some tobacco. 'Yes, can I help you?' asked the grimy looking Porto. But before he could reply, in walked a thickset Boer. The Porto immediately forgot all about the black guy and attended to the Boer. Then when he returned to him he said, "Sorry my friend, by the way what was your order?"

"Oh, me," he said. From his back pocket he took out a wad of bank notes and made as if he was counting up.

"Can I have eighteen packets of fish and chips. Hot please?"

"Eighteen fish and *mazambane*," shouted the Portuguese to the kitchen staff.

"Can I have eighteen loaves of white bread, cut into slices please and eighteen pieces of cheese put into the fish and chips."

"No, my friend," advised the Portuguese, now very respectful. "It's going to be hot and messy. Make them separate, heh?"

"Hey *wena*," shouted the shopowner to the kitchen staff. "Hurry, the gentleman is in a big hurry. Chop-chop." A black woman emerged from the kitchen carrying a huge box full of goodies.

"Is that all, my friend?" asked the Portuguese, sorting out the food and adding up.

"No," said the black guy. "Do you have Hungarian goulash?"

"What?" said the Porto. "Eh, no, no, not today," rubbing his hands and smiling.

"Well, if you don't have Hungarian goulash I can't have that food. Sorry," the black man said and dashed out of the shop before the Portuguese could fish out his gun from below the counter.

THE COFFIN WENT down, down. A thousand questions flashed in my mind. Soon it was over. People rushed to the cars. My knees could not carry me. A candle that had illuminated Soweto had been blown out. Soon it would be dark and I would get lost in the midst of it all. I wondered who could see the way?

All around I could see bright smiling faces, and yet none knew happiness. It was all a veneer. Beneath, people actually feared searching the truth.

I looked at the roads ahead of me. I knew all the roads led to the winning post, or so we all thought. Yet I could not find one I felt was taking us there.

That night, as I lay in my bed, I realized how sometimes a child is born and grows up to shine among people. Eventually when it dies it leaves a trail of blessings to those who have been fortunate enough to come closer to it. And even that makes life worth the pain.

April, 1988

Forked Tongues

IT IS REPORTED that the proceeds of the star-studded concert to be held in London on Mandela's birthday will go towards building a multi-million dollar anti-apartheid center in London. Maybe it is time we acknowledged certain feelings in the township.

The center to be built sends shivers down our spines. Does this mean the struggle of South Africa is here to stay? I remember when we were growing up, how we listened with hope to the drums of *Uhuru* beating at the borders. We felt the winds of change blowing through Africa and it seemed obvious that change would come in our lifetime. Now somehow that great momentum has come to a halt.

People in organizations that should be working to bring about our liberation have lost touch with what is happening back home. They have been away for so long that the South Africa they speak of is different from the one we know. I listened with awe to an interview with Miriam Makeba, whom I admire greatly. She spoke of people in South Africa living in hovels. Certainly when she left, the majority of blacks were living under terrible conditions. But, now, even people who live in shacks such as Mshengville would resent their dwellings being referred to as hovels.

One of the disturbing factors is that these organizations are seen as a self-sustaining industry. Another aspect is, do they really know what we want? If they are fighting for the rights of the under-privileged blacks, how do they justify the campaign against black sportsmen participating at the international level? How are we to feel when sportsmen such as Jomo Sono—our hero, a beacon of hope to millions of underprivileged boys, the pride of many a mother—is denied the right to do what he knows best? When he is denied the glory to beat the white man at his game? This is apart from denying him the right to earn a living. And what do we do? We fold our arms and let such issues pass unchallenged.

There are too many holy cows that we refuse to touch and too many blunders that have been allowed to go on because we are too scared to speak. For too long we have allowed issues that affect us go unchallenged: Sanctions, disinvestment, political inter-organizational violence, school boycotts, rent boycotts, cultural boycotts, sports boycotts, violations of human rights by the system, by liberation organizations, parents abusing children as well as children abusing parents, and much more. Everybody knows that there is a great deal of discontent over many issues but nobody dares to speak openly.

How many black people were against the "liberation now, education later" syndrome yet were not prepared to denounce it publicly? Behind the conspiracy of silence we saw a great exodus of students who went either to homelands or to private schools. How many were against the gory business of necklacing but were too scared to condemn it publicly? How often does one listen with amazement to those blacks who have become barometers of ghetto opinion speak in favor of disinvestment at white parties and say something quite different when lounging in the shebeens? How many of us have glibly lied to visiting Americans and to the embassy people in order not to be seen as moderates?

Years ago when people were still talking of calling for sanctions and disinvestment, one was impressed with statements such as, "We are prepared to suffer to achieve liberation." Yes, noble statements indeed. Unfortunately, these measures are no longer just a thought but a reality, and the tune is changing.

I listened recently to someone I hold in very high esteem speak of the impact sanctions and disinvestment already have had in this country, isolating it from the rest of the world. When I asked him where he stood, he coldly told me disinvestment was all right so long as his company was not involved. And there lies the rub.

In a country where one is immediately branded a sell-out for speaking against boycotts or sanctions, is it surprising that we choose to speak in forked tongues?

Of course we want change, and yet for that we are prepared to sacrifice not our lives but the truth. We see strategies that are bringing us nowhere nearer our liberation, but we do not speak out for fear that the Bureau of Information will be all too happy to use such statements in their favor. We do not speak out because then we will be labelled collaborators and friends of Pretoria. We suffer the pain of seeing a lot go wrong but are too chicken to voice our opinions in public.

There is a myth that because we are anti-government, therefore we must unquestioningly be pro any measure imposed by the movements. Everybody knows that this is not in fact true. We are against the government and the System and are also against school boycotts and necklacing. Even the children know this. Everybody states his view strongly to his neighbor, but if we are asked for a public view we all suddenly toe the line.

We want liberations and not reforms. Many of us have said and mean that we are prepared to die for liberation. But we do not want to die by being necklaced or by burning people's homes. Nor do we want to increase the number of martyrs. We are prepared to be part of real change. Cosmetics, reforms and all such half measures are not the change we want. But we do not think the present strategies go anywhere towards bringing about successful revolution. We are prepared to follow our leaders to the bush so that our children and those who will come after us can be free, but we must believe that the leaders know where they are leading us.

We want the government pressurized, and not bolstered. We want pressure to be brought against the system, but we want that pressure to be effective, not just harmful. When liberation comes it should find us prepared, something we cannot be without jobs or education. To the majority of us, the struggle is not something we fantasize about. When Jomo Sono speaks of being part of the oppressed majority he is not echoing an empty slogan. He has had to struggle as a black boy and a black man in this country to reach world acclaim.

As black people in this country we live the struggle in the ghetto every day of our lives. We know the effects of receiving an inferior education. We know what it is to be first fired and last hired. We witness black students coming out of high schools with meaningless matric certificates. When we raise such issues we are not trying to score points; we want the situation corrected. For how long are we to keep quiet as other people, some of whom are without the vaguest idea of what we want, speak on our behalf?

If history will judge the present youth harshly for the blunders it has incurred, then it will judge the adults even more harshly for not leading when they were supposed to.

May, 1988

Glossary

NOTE: Words in the definitions that are set in SMALL CAPS are also found elsewhere in the glossary.

"ABELUNGU NQO DAMN BASIBIZA NQOJIM." A workers' song, much like songs sung by American prison chain gangs. Sung mainly by gold miners. Rhythm of the phrasing helps keep time with digging.

AFRIKAANS. Language of the AFRIKANERS living in South Africa.

AFRIKANERS. Often called the "white tribe of Africa"; the descendants of the first Dutch settlers to arrive with JAN VAN RIEBEECK in what is now Cape Town in 1652.

AUS. Afrikaans abbreviation for the word *oussie*, meaning "sister."

AZAPO. (Azanian People's Organization); founded 1977; heir to the BLACK CONSCIOUSNESS MOVEMENT begun by Steve Biko; major rival of UNITED DEMOCRATIC FRONT (UDF). Azania is the black nationalist name for a future black-controlled South Africa.

AZASM. (Azanian Students Movement), called the "Zim-Zims." Mainly high-school-age students who are oriented toward the philosophy of the BLACK CONSCIOUSNESS MOVEMENT.

BABBELAASED. Hung over.

BALUNGUS. Zulu, "white people."

BANTU. Zulu word originally meaning "people." In South African vocabulary, it means "black people."

BANTU EDUCATION. A system of education designed by the government for blacks, separate from education planning and development for whites, Coloureds and Indians. After the 1976 student revolts, the government changed the name Bantu Education to DEPARTMENT OF EDUCATION AND TRAINING (DET). Education for blacks is inferior, putting them, generally, outside the benefits of higher education.

BARAGWANATH. Largest hospital in South Africa, located in SOWETO on the OLD POTCHEFSTROOM ROAD.

BAZALWANE. Zulu, "church congregation."

BEKKERSDAL. A township which was the scene of massive political uprisings in 1985.

BETERKOFFIE. Someone with a chip on his/her shoulder.

BLACK CHRISTMAS BOYCOTT. As a means of protest, blacks in townships of South Africa, particularly in SOWETO, boycott stores owned and operated by whites during the Christmas season.

BLACK CONSCIOUSNESS MOVEMENT. A political movement founded in the early 1970s by black university students disenchanted with white norms and practices. The idea and movement were founded upon a basic belief that blacks must address their own shortcomings, understand their own unique history and place in southern Africa and act on their own behalf, without assistance from well-meaning white liberals. Black Consciousness organizations were banned in 1977 following the death in detention of the best-known proponent, Steve Biko.

BLACK MARIA. A Government van that collects corpses from the townships. Hospital ambulances will not transport corpses outside SOWETO. Interestingly, these vans are never black in color.

BOERS. Literally, "farmers" in AFRIKAANS. Blacks in South Africa apply the term to all AFRIKANERS.

P.W. BOTHA. State president of the Republic of South Africa; formerly prime minister and minister of defence.

BOTTLE STORE. Liquor store.

BRA. Common South African term for "brother." Usage denotes respect.

BUSH. The VELD regions.

BISHOP MANAS BUTHELEZI. Well-known Lutheran bishop.

CAROL. The author, Nomavenda Mathiane, was born in the homeland of Venda to Zulu parents. Her father was an officer in the Salvation Army. Nomavenda was also given the name "Carol" as her Christian name.

CASSPIRS. Heavily armed trucks used by the SOUTH AFRICAN DEFENCE FORCES (SADF).

CHIAWELLO 1, 2 & 3. This is a SOWETO township divided into three sections, called "extensions."

COLOURED. A South African government classification referring to persons of mixed race. There are four classifications: "white," "Coloured," "Indian/Asian" and "black."

COMBIS. Mini-buses used to transport eight to twelve people.

COMMITTEE OF TEN. Founded in 1977 following the arrests of SOWETO civic leaders; created by the *Weekend World* newspaper before it was officially banned and disbanded; however short-lived, it did manage to create the Soweto Civic Association, which was to play a leading role in the rent boycotts of 1986.

COMRADES. Bands of youths, claiming to be activists, who in reality are roaming criminal gangs. Also referred to as SAYINYOVAS, or "disturbers," "disruptives."

COM-TSOTSIS. Tsotsis are hooligans, muggers, street rabble. Com-tsotsis are those comrades who behave like Tsotsis, hence a combination of the two words.

COSATU. (Congress of South African Trade Unions); headquarters bombed in 1987 during the SATS strike.

CRECHE. Nursery school or kindergarten.

CREDO MUTWA. A pseudo artist, SANGOMA and author, residing in SOWETO.

DECEMBER 16. AFRIKANERS mark this date as the Day of the Covenant or the Day of the Vow. On this day, in 1838, Andreis Pretorius led the BOERS to defeat a massive Zulu army led by Chief Dingane in the Battle of Blood River. Previously called Dingane's Day. December 16 is celebrated as an annual, national holiday or memorial day by AFRIKANERS.

DET. (Department of Education and Training); office overseeing education for blacks in South Africa; see BANTU EDUCATION.

DIEPKLOOF. Persons removed from the Alexander township were relocated to the Diepkloof township.

DUBE BRIDGE INCIDENT. In 1965, the Dube train station bridge collapsed, killing or permanently injuring a large number of commuters.

EAST LONDON. A port city on the eastern coast of South Africa (on the Indian Ocean).

ECC. (End Conscription Campaign); anti-draft organization now banned by the South African government.

ELDORADO. A township area southeast of Johannesburg where Coloureds reside.

EMNDENI. A township in Soweto.

FREEDOM CHARTER. In June 1955 the ANC joined other principal anti-apartheid groups in creating the Congress Alliance. They formulated the Freedom Charter, which set down principles and guidelines for the struggle for South African democracy. It was hailed by blacks as a major step forward and condemned by most whites as a recipe for Marxist revolution and disaster.

GA-RANKUA. A township outside PRETORIA.

GEYSER. A device for keeping water heated.

GEZINA. A railway station in SOWETO.

GIYANI. A township in Gazankulu, a homeland for the Shangaans tribe.

GREAT TREASON TRIAL. See RIVONIA TRIAL.

GROUP AREAS ACT. The government decree defining where racial groups could and could not live.

GUY FAWKES CRACKERS. Fire works, small explosives.

HAMMANSKRAAL. A black residential area outside PRETORIA where a Catholic seminary is located. Seminars were held there by Steve Biko, leader of the BLACK CONSCIOUSNESS MOVEMENT.

177

HARARE. Capital city of Zimbabwe; formerly Salisbury, capital city of Rhodesia.

HARRY SAM. A notorious Greek cafe owner in Braamfontein who is said to have a hot temper..

HOMELANDS. Under the apartheid system, as established by the National Party beginning in 1948, ten homelands were to become national, independent "states" for blacks in South Africa. To date, four are "independent" (recognized by only the South African government): Transkei, Bophuthatswana, Ciskei and Venda. The others are Lebowa, KwaNdebele, Gazankulu, KaNgwane, QwaQwa and KwaZulu.

HOSTEL INMATE. Hostels are single-sex sleeping quarters for black workers in urban areas. Families are generally not permitted to live with male or female workers who commute into white areas for long-term or short-term employment.

IMPI. Zulu, "warrior."

INYANGA. Zulu word for "spiritualist" or "diviner"; similar to a SANGOMA.

JABAVU. See WHITE CITY (JABAVU).

LEABUA JONATHAN. Prime minister of Lesotho deposed in 1985.

"JOU SKELEM." "You scoundrel." AFRIKAANS expression used freely among many groups. Can be used in friendly jest or as a derogatory exclamation.

JUNE 16. See SOWETO 1976.

KAFFIR. Originally an Arab term meaning "non-believer," now used by South African whites to mean "nigger."

"KAWUFANE UCINGE." Xhosa phrase meaning "just imagine."

KHAYA. Zulu, "home."

KLIPSPRUIT. A township in SOWETO next to PIMVILLE.

KRUGER DAY. A national day honoring Paul Kruger, state president in 1883.

LAAGER. AFRIKAANS word meaning an encircled camp. The original AFRIKANER settlers would make camp by forming their wagons in a tight circle, presenting an invulnerable front to any would-be attackers.

POTLAKO LEBALLO. PAN-AFRICANIST CONGRESS (PAC) leader who died in exile.

LEKTON HOUSE. Headquarters of the trade unions affiliated with the BLACK CONSCIOUSNESS MOVEMENT, located in Johannesburg.

LEMBEDE MDA FOUNDATION. Named after Anton Lembede and A.P. Mda who were members of the ANC Youth League and founders of the Pan Africanist Congress. The foundation supports community projects such as literacy classes among hostel dwellers. Members also explain the legal system to clients, assist in paperwork to purchase houses, etc.

LENASIA. Indian township area located south of Johannesburg.

LENZ. Indian township outside SOWETO.

LUSAKA. Capital of Zambia and headquarters of the exiled African National Congress (ANC).

SAMORA MACHEL. Late president of Mozambique (died in a plane crash in South African territory in 1986).

MADAM/MASTER. Formal address used by black workers when speaking to white employers.

MAHHALA. Zulu, "for free" or "for nothing."

MAKABASA. The name of a gang operating in SOWETO. Rumored to be allied with one of the many political groups in the townships, their main activity was stealing cars.

DANIEL FRANÇOIS MALAN. Nationalist party leader, 1933-1954; prime minister of South Africa, 1939-1948.

MAMATHIANE. Sotho prefix used for respectful address, "Mrs. Mathiane."

NELSON MANDELA. Black nationalist leader, symbolic head of the African National Congress (ANC) and founder of ANC paramilitary wing, Umkhonto we Sizwe (Spear of the Nation). Imprisoned since 1964.

"MANENE NAMANENEKAZI." Xhosa phrase meaning "Ladies and Gentlemen."

MAPETLA. Township in SOWETO.

MATRIC. Final examinations at high school level, qualifying passing candidates for university study.

MAZAMBANE. Zulu, "potatoes."

MAZISTA BRICKS. Inexpensive building blocks used for cheap, rapid construction of housing.

GOVAN MBEKI. Imprisoned ANC leader released in 1987.

MEADOWLANDS. Persons removed from the Sophiatown area were relocated to the Meadowlands township.

MIDWAY. The railway station following CHIAWELLO station in SOWETO.

MIELIE MEAL. Cornmeal, pap.

MITCHELL'S PLAIN. A Coloured township outside of Cape Town.

MIXED MARRIAGES ACT. A government decree forbidding official, legal marriage between members of different racial groups. This act was recently repealed.

JOHNSON MLAMBO. Exiled PAC leader.

MOLAPO. A township in SOWETO.

MOSHOESHOE. A Mesotho leader of the Basotho people who established his kingdom in what is now Lesotho. Can also be spelled "Moshweshwe."

M PLAN. Attempt to organize independent, local self-government in the townships in 1953. Called the "M Plan" because the initiator was said to have been NELSON MANDELA. Organizing neighborhoods into block committees and STREET COMMITTEES got its start at that time.

DR. ROBERT MUGABE. Prime minister of Zimbabwe since 1980.

NALEDI. A township in SOWETO.

NAMIBIA. Southwest Africa; territory claimed by South Africa but disputed by United Nations in Resolution 435.

"NANKAMAHIPPO." *Hippo* is the nickname for a type of military truck used to transport soldiers into the townships. *"Nankamahippo!"* is Zulu for, "Here come the hippos!"

NATIONAL FORUM. Meeting in 1985 of organizations opposed to the newly formed tricameral Parliament in South Africa.

NECKLACE. A car/truck tire placed around the body of an intended victim, which is then set alight with gasoline (petrol). It has been used to execute alleged informers, collaborators and anyone else thought to be cooperating with the South African governmental authorities. The height of the necklacing was between 1985 and 1986.

NEW CANADA. A railroad "T" junction just before entering SOWETO.

BISHOP SIMEON NKOANE. Anglican Bishop of Johannesburg.

NYOVMENT. Disturbance; from Zulu word *nyova*, meaning "to disrupt."

OLD POTCHEFSTROOM ROAD. One of the main roads running through Soweto; also known as the Old Potch Road; before the advent of major highways, this was the main road leading from SOWETO to Potchefstroom.

OPERATION HUNGER. A project of the South African Institute of Race Relations; campaign primarily directed at feeding the hungry in the homelands; activities include soup kitchens and agricultural programs.

ORLANDO. One of the oldest townships in SOWETO.

OU. AFRIKAANS slang for "guy" or "fellow."

OUPA. AFRIKAANS for "grandfather" or "grandpa."

PAC. (Pan-Africanist Congress); founded by DR. ROBERT SOBUKWE in 1959; African nationalists who broke with the ANC; established the idea of BLACK CONSCIOUSNESS, which rejects cooperation with and identification with white liberals or radicals.

PAP. Cornmeal, the staple diet for blacks.

PAW-PAW. Fruit with a soft, watery inner core and a tough outer skin

PFP. (Progressive Federal Party); the liberal opposition party, to the left of the National Party; advocates a qualified franchise within a federal government structure; support comes from fairly affluent, English-speaking voters.

PHOMOLONG. A township in SOWETO.

PIETERSBURG. A town located in the northern Transvaal province near the Zimbabwe border.

PIMVILLE. A township in SOWETO.

POLLSMOOR. Large prison in Cape Town where NELSON MANDELA was interned from 1982 to 1988.

PORT ELIZABETH. A port city on the eastern coast of South Africa (on the Indian Ocean).

PORTO. A derogatory reference to a Portuguese person.

PRETORIA. Seat of the government of South Africa. Cape Town is the seat of parliament and Bloemfontein is the location of the judicial branch of the government.

PRETORIA MAXIMUM PRISON. Located in Pretoria, the administrative capital of South Africa. This is where most executions take place.

PUNTER PASTOR. Pastor who bets on the horses.

PUTCO. (Public Utility Transport Corporation); bus service company operating in all urban areas of South Africa.

RAND. As of 8 December 1988, the South African currency stood at 2.05 Rand per U.S. dollar; to calculate U.S. dollar amount, multiply Rand figure by .48554.

REGINA MUNDI. "Queen of the World" (or "Queen of the Earth"); largest cathedral in South Africa, located in Rockville township. Most political commemoration services and funeral services for political activists and important SOWETO personalities are held here.

JAN VAN RIEBEECK. Employee of the Dutch East India Company who opened a re-supply station in what is now Cape Town in 1652. Established first white, Dutch colony in Southern Africa.

RIVONIA TRIAL. Seven-month trial without a jury ending in June 1964; eight leaders of Umkhonto we Sizwe (Spear of the Nation, the paramilitary wing of the ANC), including NELSON MANDELA, were found guilty of sabotage and conspiracy and sentenced to life imprisonment. The results of this trial were to have a devastating effect on the BLACK NATIONALIST MOVEMENT, which lost some of its most effective leaders.

ROBBEN ISLAND. Island prison off the shore of Cape Town where male inmates are held. First used to hold political prisoners during British colonial rule of South Africa. Many famous detainees have been held on the island over the past several decades, including ROBERT SOBUKWE and NELSON MANDELA.

ROCKVILLE. A township in SOWETO.

RUFARO. A stadium in HARARE, the capital of Zimbabwe, where independence celebrations were held, April 1980.

SADF. (South African Defence Forces).

SANGOMA. Zulu, "diviner"; an indigenous "faith healer." Can be male or female.

SARWHU. (South African Railway and Harbor Workers' Union).

SATS. (South African Transport Service).

SAYINYOVA. Zulu, "disturber," "disrupter."

SCA. (Soweto Civic Association); see STREET COMMITTEES.

SENAOANE. A township in SOWETO.

SHARPEVILLE. On 21 March 1960, sixty-nine blacks were shot during a demonstration (most of them in the back) in Sharpeville, a township located outside Johannesburg to the southeast. The original demonstration was organized by the newly formed PAN-AFRICANIST CONGRESS (founded in 1959 by DR. ROBERT SO-BUKWE) to protest the pass laws.

SHEBEEN. Private home used as an unlicensed bar and liquor store.

SHIBUKU. African sorghum beer.

DAVID SIBEKO. A leading member of the PAN-AFRICANIST CONGRESS (PAC) murdered in Dar-es-Salaam (Tanzania) in 1979.

ALBERTINA SISULU. Co-vice-president of the UDF. Wife of ANC leader Walter Sisulu and mother of editor (*The New Nation*) Zwelakhe Sisulu.

WALTER SISULU. Imprisoned ANC leader.

SIYAYINYOVA. To disrupt. Comrades on the move would sing *"Siyayinyova, Oh! Siyayinyova!"*

SJAMBOK. A long whip, generally having a metal tip used mainly by "vigilantes" and rural police. To *sjambok* someone is to whip him.

JAN CHRISTIAAN SMUTS. Prime minister of South Africa 1919-1924, and 1939-1948.

ROBERT SOBUKWE. Founder of the PAN-AFRICANIST CONGRESS (1959); died in internal exile in 1978.

SOSCO. (South African Students Congress); a high school age student organization oriented toward the philosophy of the UNITED DEMOCRATIC FRONT (UDF).

SOWETO. (SOuth WEstern TOwnships); a combination of twenty-six small towns with some 2 million inhabitants (official count is 900,000). What is now Soweto came into being after gold was discovered in the late nineteenth century outside Johannesburg in the Witswatersrand. By 1963, it was a series of shantytowns built by blacks who were not permitted to reside within the city limits.

SOWETO 1976. Wednesday, 16 June 1976, marked a turning point in black township protest against the ruling AFRIKANER (National Party) government. Some 20,000 schoolchildren protesting the enforced use of AFRIKAANS in their classrooms, marched on SOWETO schools. By the end of the week, some 176 students and adults had been shot. Revolt spread quickly throughout the country. One result of the uprising was the strengthening of the BLACK CONSCIOUSNESS MOVEMENT.

SOWETO ELEVEN. Ten male and one female students charged with inciting the 16 June 1976 student revolt in SOWETO. All eleven were detained for two years; some were eventually acquitted, while others served prison sentences (the males on ROBBEN ISLAND and the one female in Potschefstroom Prison, one of South Africa's prisons for women).

SOWETO URBAN COUNCIL. The administrative body governing SOWETO.

SRC. (Students Representative Council).

STAYAWAYS. Boycott period when SOWETO residents stay at home instead of going to workplaces or school in Johannesburg.

STREET COMMITTEE. With the collapse of law and order in 1986, local neighborhood authority was established, principally to assist individuals facing eviction because of their participation in rent boycotts. A street committee comprised six to ten streets in a neighborhood, each with a representative. These leaders formed the Soweto Civic Association (SCA). Street committees had a wide range of ideological differences, depending upon the political/philosophical orientation of the local representatives.

Johannes G. Strydom (or Strijdom). Prime minister of South Africa, 1954-1958.

Helen Suzman. Leading member of the Progressive Federal Party (PFP); member of House of Assembly (parliament) for thirty-five years. For many years, the sole opposition voice in parliament.

Oliver Tambo. President of the exiled ANC.

Tembisa. A black township located next to Jan Smuts International Airport.

Thaba Bosiu. A large mountain in Lesotho, scene of many tribal battles.

Thokoza. A township in East Rand.

Tladi. A township in Soweto.

Transvaal. One of the four provinces of South Africa (Transvaal, Orange Free State, Natal and the Cape).

Tsotsi/Mfundisi. Literally, "minister-cum-thug" in Zulu.

Ubuntu. Zulu, "humanity" or "humaneness."

UDF. (United Democratic Front); founded 1983; largest anti-apartheid organization composed of some 700 large and small groups; multi-racial membership.

Uhuru. Originally a Kenyan word meaning "freedom," now in general use throughout the African continent.

UMLAZI. A township near Durban (Natal Province).

VAAL RIVER. Divides the Transvaal from the Orange Free State, two of the four provinces of South Africa. The township of Lekoa (Sotho word for the Vaal River), in the Vaal area, was the site of the first rent boycotts.

VELD. A grasslands plateau located in the Orange Free State between the Drakensburg mountain range and the Eastern Cape; Afrikaans word meaning "empty space" or "uninhabited."

VENDA. Name of both a tribe and a homeland in South Africa. One of the four main linguistic divisions of blacks in the region (Nguni, Sotho, Tsonga and Venda). The Venda tribe inhabits areas below the Limpopo River; flanked by Zimbabweans to the north and the Shangaans to the south.

HENRIK FRENSCH VERWOERD. Prime minister of South Africa, 1958-1966; implemented racial segregation laws (apartheid); took South Africa out of the British Commonwealth; assassinated in Parliament's House of Assembly.

VOORTREKKERHOOGTE. An army base outside PRETORIA.

VUSI. Zulu, "to rebuild the house." Shortened version of full word, *vusumuzi*. Also used as a first name.

WARARAS. This student group leans more toward the African National Congress (ANC); BLACK CONSCIOUSNESS adherents call ANC members "charterists" because they purportedly support the tenets of the 1955 FREEDOM CHARTER. *Warwara* comes from the AFRIKAANS word *waar* which means "where." The inference here is, "Where do the Wararas or 'charterists' stand?"

WENA. Zulu, "you."

WEST RAND ADMINISTRATION BOARD. The board that preceded the SoWETO URBAN COUNCIL administering the twenty-six townships comprising SOWETO. Before being named the West Rand Administrative Board (WRAB), it was called the Non-European Affairs Department.

WHITE CITY (JABAVU). A township in SOWETO next to Rockville; low income area. Jabavu is named after Dr. Tengo Jabavu, a renowned South African scholar.

WITS. University of Witwatersrand, located in Johannesburg.

YELLOW MELLOW. Police bus whose front and side windows are wire mesh. Children gave the bus this name (which is also the name of a favorite soft drink) because of its yellow color.

ZOLA. A township in SOWETO.

ZULULAND. KwaZulu homeland located in the province of Natal. Majority of Zulus live in this eastern region bordering on the Indian Ocean.

ZWIDE. A township in Port Elizabeth.

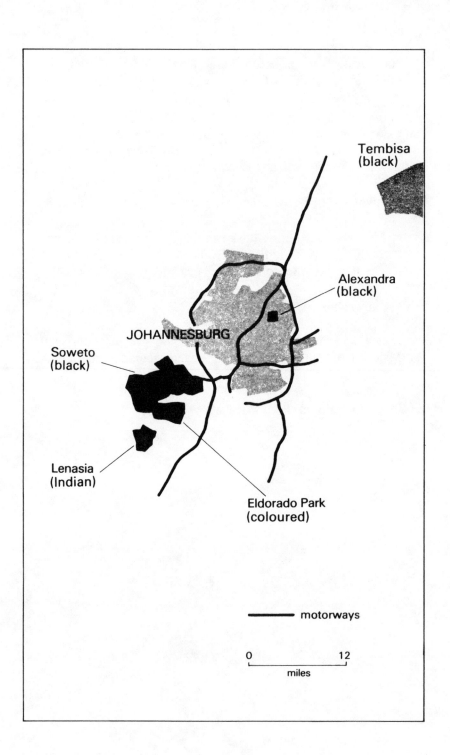

Tembisa
(black)

Alexandra
(black)

JOHANNESBURG

Soweto
(black)

Lenasia
(Indian)

Eldorado Park
(coloured)

motorways

0   12
miles

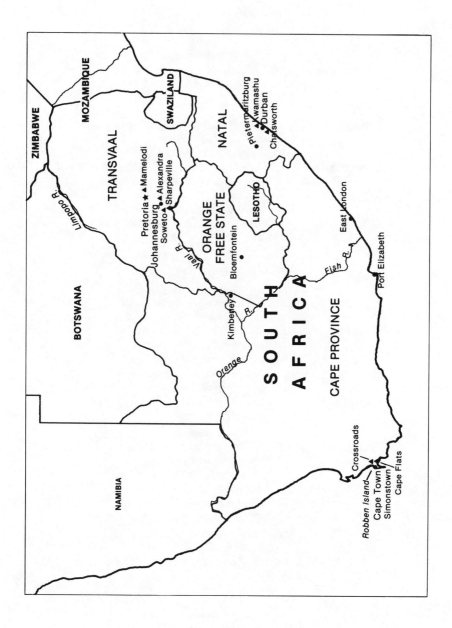

FREEDOM HOUSE BOOKS

General Editor: James Finn

YEARBOOKS

Freedom in the World: Political Rights and Civil Liberties,
Raymond D. Gastil; annuals from 1978-1988.

STUDIES IN FREEDOM

Escape to Freedom: The Story of the International Rescue Committee,
Aaron Levenstein; 1983.

Forty Years: A Third World Soldier at the UN,
Carlos P. Romulo (with Beth Day Romulo); 1986. *(Romulo: A Third World Soldier at the UN,* paperback edition, 1987.)

Today's American: How Free?
James Finn & Leonard R. Sussman, (Eds.); 1986.

Will of the People: Original Democracies in Non-Western Societies,
Raul S. Manglapus; 1987.

PERSPECTIVES ON FREEDOM

Three Years at the East-West Divide,
Max M. Kampelman; (Introductions by Ronald Reagan and Jimmy Carter; edited by Leonard R. Sussman); 1983.

The Democratic Mask: The Consolidation of the Sandinista Revolution,
Douglas W. Payne; 1985.

The Heresy of Words in Cuba: Freedom of Expression & Information,
Carlos Ripoll; 1985.

Human Rights & the New Realism: Strategic Thinking in a New Age,
Michael Novak; 1986.

To License A Journalist?,
Inter-American Court of Human Rights; 1986.

The Catholic Church in China,
L. Ladany; 1987.

Glasnost: How Open?
Soviet & Eastern European Dissidents; 1987.

Yugoslavia: The Failure of "Democratic" Communism; 1987.

The Prague Spring: A Mixed Legacy
Jiri Pehe, ed. 1988.

Romania: A Case of "Dynastic" Communism; 1989.